BAY COUNTY AREA SCHOOLS
SAND LAKE ELEMENTARY

Student Edition:

Expressions Music Curriculum™, Music Expressions™, Band Expressions™, Jazz Expressions™, Orchestra Expressions™, Choral Expressions™, Piano Expressions™, and Guitar Expressions™ are trademarks of Warner Bros. Publications. All Rights Reserved.

2 3 4 5 6 7 8 9 10   08 07 06 05 04 03

© 2003 WARNER BROS. PUBLICATIONS U.S. INC.
All Rights Reserved

Any duplication, adaptation or arrangement of the compositions contained in this publication requires the consent of the Publisher. No part of this publication may be photocopied or reproduced in any way without permission. Unauthorized uses are an infringement of the U.S. Copyright Act and are punishable thereunder.

Warner Bros. Publications • 15800 NW 48th Avenue • Miami, FL 33014

COMPLETE TEACHER EDITION (EMC2001)
UPC: 6-54979-05504-4
ISBN: 0-7579-1045-9 90000

TEACHER EDITION, VOLUME I (EMC2001A)
UPC: 6-54979-05496-2
ISBN: 0-7579-1037-8 90000

TEACHER EDITION, VOLUME II (EMC2001B)
UPC: 6-54979-05497-9
ISBN: 0-7579-1038-6 90000

TEACHER EDITION, VOLUME III (EMC2001C)
UPC: 6-54979-05498-6
ISBN: 0-7579-1039-4 90000

TEACHER EDITION, VOLUME IV (EMC2001D)
UPC: 6-54979-05499-3
ISBN: 0-7579-1040-8 90000

STUDENT BOOK (EMC2002)
UPC: 6-54979-05500-6
ISBN: 0-7579-1041-6 90000

Credits

PROJECT CREATORS & COORDINATORS
Robert W. Smith
Susan L. Smith

PROJECT EDITOR
Judith M. Stoehr

AUTHORS
Judith M. Stoehr
Lead Author
Creative Insights
Omaha, Nebraska

June M. Hinckley
Department of Education
Tallahassee, Florida

Darla S. Hanley, Ph.D.
Shenandoah University
Winchester, Virginia

Carolyn C. Minear
Orange County Public Schools
Orlando, Florida

CONTRIBUTING AUTHORS
Timothy S. Brophy, Ph.D.
Assessment Specialist
University of Florida
Gainesville, Florida

Art Williams
Media Specialist
Troy, Alabama

CONSULTANTS
June M. Hinckley
National Standards for the Arts Consultant
Department of Education
Tallahassee, Florida

James Clarke
Fine Art Consultant
Executive Director
Texas Coalition for Quality Arts Education
Houston, Texas

Kathy Robinson
Multicultural Consultant
Eastman School of Music
Rochester, New York

David Peters
Technology Coordinator
University of Indiana
Indianapolis, Indiana

Doug Brasell
Website Coordinator
Cairo, Georgia

Artie Almeida
Listening Maps
Bear Lake Elementary School
Apopka, Florida

MULTICULTURAL AMBASSADORS & CONTRIBUTORS
Toshio Akayama
Professor Emeritus
Musashino School of Music
Tokyo, Japan

Kathy Robinson
Eastman School of Music
Rochester, New York

Kyung-Ah Gina Moon
African-American Research Library and Cultural Center
Fort Lauderdale, Florida

Min Xie Shaheen
Miami, Florida

Emma Perennes
New York, New York

ORCHESTRA
Michael L. Alexander
Houston, Texas

Gerald E. Anderson
Los Angeles, California

Kathleen DeBarry Brungard
Charlotte, North Carolina

Sandra Dackow
Trenton, New Jersey

Anne C. Witt
Tuscaloosa, Alabama

BAND
Jim Campbell
Lexington, Kentucky

Richard C. Crain
The Woodlands, Texas

Linda Gammon
Fairfax, Virginia

Gary Markham
Atlanta, Georgia

Michael Story
Houston, Texas

JAZZ
J. Richard Dunscomb
Atlanta, Georgia

Jose Diaz
Houston, Texas

Dr. Willie L. Hill, Jr.
Amherst, Massachusetts

Jerry Tolson
Louisville, Kentucky

CHORAL
Dr. Darla S. Hanley
Winchester, Virginia

Jim Kimmell
Nashville, Tennessee

Dr. Russ Robinson
Gainesville, Florida

Jerry Tolson
Louisville, Kentucky

CONTRIBUTORS
Pilot and Practicing Teachers:

Kara Bell, *Great Falls, MT*
Cheryl Black, *Camden, SC*
W. Elaine Blocher, *Derby, KS*
Karen Bouton, *Graceville, FL*
Patty Brennan, *Chesapeake, VA*
Temetia Creed, *Tampa, FL*
Scott T. Evans, *Orlando, FL*
Debbie Fahmie, *Kissimmee, FL*
David Fox, *Oviedo, FL*
Mary Gibson, *Maitland, FL*
Claudette Gray, *Pittsburgh, PA*
Lisa Hamer, *Moncks Corner, SC*
Julie Harmon, *North Platte, NE*
Jennifer Hartman, *Shawnee, KS*
Elaine Hashem, *Penacook, NH*
Mark Hodges, *Sumter, SC*
Beverly Holl, *Los Angeles, CA*
Grace Jordan, *Orlando, FL*
Lyn Koch, *Pittsburgh, PA*
Eunice Marrero, *Orlando, FL*
Nancy McBride, *Anderson, SC*
Kathleen Scott Meske, *Los Angeles, CA*
Deborah Mosier, *Bennington, NE*
Debi Noel, *Eugene, OR*
Keisha C. Pendergrass, *Clover, SC*
Teresa Sims, *Troy, AL*
Marjorie Smith, *Lutz, FL*
Lisa Stern, *Winter Park, FL*
Julie A. Swank, *Troy, OH*
Jane Wall, *Wexford, PA*
Kirsten H. Wilcox, *Winchester, VA*
Leslie A. Wooten, *LaGrange, KY*

RECORDING
Robert Dingley
Executive Producer

Robert W. Smith
Producer

Jack Lamb
Associate Producer

Kendall Thomsen
Recording Engineer

Andy de Ganahl
Mix Engineer

Jason May
Mix Engineer

MUSIC ARRANGING
Robert W. Smith
Michael Story
Jack Bullock
Victor Lopez
Timothy S. Brophy

Don Beattie
Piano Accompaniments

Delayna Beattie
Piano Accompaniments

WARNER BROS. PUBLICATIONS
Fred Anton
CEO

Robert Dingley
Vice President: Education

David Hakim
Vice President: Sales

Andrea Nelson
Vice President: Marketing

Lourdes Carreras-Balepogi
Marketing Coordinator

David Olsen
Director, Business Affairs

PRODUCTION
Thom Proctor
Project Manager

Gayle Giese
Production Editor

Bill Galliford
Music Arranging Assistance

Donna Wheeler
Editorial Assistance

Heather Mahone
Editorial Assistance

Susan Buckey
Editorial Assistance

Nadine DeMarco
Text Proofreader

Joy Galliford
Text Proofreader

Nancy Rehm
Senior Art Director

Shawn Martinez
Assisant Art Director

Thais Yanes
Student Book Page Layout

Al Nigro
Music Engraving Manager

Mark Young
Music Engraver

Glenda Mikell
Music Engraver

Glyn Dryhurst
Director, Production Services

Hank Fields
Production Coordinator

Sharon Marlow
Production Assistance

Credits

TEACHER EDITION INTERIOR LAYOUT

InterMedia
A Mad 4 Marketing Company

Margaret Stapleton
Project Director

Anne Rogers
Production Coordinator

Marie LaFauci
Senior Artist

Amy Wertzler

Maureen Hyman

Leo Jones

Dana Kaufman

Elyse Taylor

Roque Rodón

Linda Smith

Michelle M. White

ACKNOWLEDGMENTS
Thanks to:

Estefan Enterprises for providing photographs of Gloria Estefan on pages 106–107.

Kyung-Ah Gina Moon for the Korean to English translation and pronunciation for "Haak Gyo Jong."

Emma Perennes for the French Cajun to English translation and pronunciation for "Saute, Crapaud!"

Min Xie Shaheen for the English to Chinese translation and pronunciation guide for "Hao Peng You."

Barbara Zimmerman, President: BZ/Rights & Permissions, Inc., for the work in securing the rights and permissions for the fine art and photographs.

Donald Norsworthy, for photography of Mr. Art and Music Expressions™ characters.

West Music, for use of instrument photos.

Steve Palm, Vice President, Scholastic Marketing Partners, Scholastic Inc., for marketing consultation.

Gino Silva, Art Director, Scholastic Marketing Partners, Scholastic Inc., for cover and logo designs.

Scholastic Inc. for the use of the story "Cucarachita Martina" from *Señor Cat's Romance and Other Favorite Stories From Latin America* retold by Lucia M. Gonzalez. Published by Scholastic Press, a division of Scholastic Inc. Copyright © 1997 by Lucia M. Gonzalez. Used by permission of Scholastic Inc.

Adrian Alvarez for Spanish translation editing of "Ambos a Dos" and "El Juego Chirimbolo."

Corbis® for the photograph of Ray Charles on Student Edition page 8. © www.corbis.com/CORBIS.

The Florida Philharmonic Orchestra & Chorus, Joseph Silverstein, Acting Music Director, for the photo of the adult chorus on page 51.

The Greater Miami Symphonic Band for the concert band photo on page 50.

GIA Publications for the photo of a girl playing the French horn on page 51. © GIA Publications, Inc., Chicago, Illinois. All rights reserved. Used by permission.

ILLUSTRATION CREDITS
(Student Edition page/Teacher Edition page)

1/4. Martha Ramirez

2–3/5. Janel Harrison

4–5/6. Thais Yanes

6–7/7. Robert Ramsay/Janel Harrison

8–9/8. Joe Klucar

10–11/9. Ernesto Ebanks

12–13/12–13. Martha Ramirez

14–15/20. Natalie Auth

16–17/21. Magdi Rodriguez

19/23. Candy Woolley

20–21/28. Janel Harrison

22–23/30. Jeannette Aquino

24–25/30. Martha Ramirez

26–27/30. Olivia Novak

28–29/32. Candy Woolley

31/33. Jeannette Aquino

32–33/37. Jeannette Aquino

34–35/38. Jeannette Aquino

36–37/39. Ken Rehm

38–39/45. Thais Yanes

40–41/46. Nancy Rehm

44–45/48. Nancy Rehm

46–47/52. Nancy Rehm

48–49/55, 120. Robert Ramsay

50–51/55. Joe Klucar

52–53/61, 87. Ernesto Ebanks

54–55/61. Ernesto Ebanks

56–57/63. Joe Klucar

58–59/68. Ernesto Ebanks

60–61/70, 76. Jeannette Aquino

62–63/71. Jeannette Aquino

64–65/77. Nancy Rehm

66–67/79. Magdi Rodriguez

70–71/85. Candy Woolley

72–73/90. Nancy Rehm

74–75/92, 279. Thais Yanes

76–77/93. Thais Yanes

79/93. Jeannette Aquino

80–81/95. Jeannette Aquino

82–83/95. Jeannette Aquino

84–85/101. Joe Klucar

86–87/102. Joe Klucar

90–91/111. Martha Ramirez

92–93/111, 151. Martha Ramirez

94–95/112. Martha Ramirez

96–97/117. Ken Rehm

99/118. Nancy Rehm

100–101/126. Magdi Rodriguez

102–103/126. Magdi Rodriguez

106–107/144. Candy Woolley

108–109/145. Ernesto Ebanks

110–111/147. Jeannette Aquino

112–113/152. Candy Woolley

115/154. Ken Rehm

116–117/158. Candy Woolley

119/161. Nancy Rehm

121/168. Robert Ramsay

122–123/172. Jeannette Aquino

124–125/174. Olivia Novak

126–127/175. Candy Woolley

128–129/176. Lisa Greene Mane

130–131/178. Joe Klucar

132–133/178. Joe Klucar

135/179. Candy Woolley

136–137/185. Shawn Martinez/Candy Woolley

139/188. Thais Yanes

140–141/194. Ken Rehm

142–143/195. Ken Rehm

144–145/195. Nancy Rehm

146–147/196. Jeannette Aquino

148–149/203. Jeannette Aquino

150–151/203. Natalie Auth

152–153/205. Jeannette Aquino

155/211. Jeannette Aquino

156–157/212. Candy Woolley

158–159/217. Thais Yanes

160–161/217. Candy Woolley

162–163/219. Jeannette Aquino

164–165/219. Jeannette Aquino

166–167/232. Lisa Greene Mane

168–169/233. Ernesto Ebanks

170–171/235. Lisa Greene Mane

172–173/236. Lisa Greene Mane

174–175/243. Jeannette Aquino

176–177/245. Magdi Rodriguez

178–179/246. Lisa Greene Mane

180–181/246. Magdi Rodriguez

182–183/248. Candy Woolley

184/254. Olivia Novak

186–187/271. Jeannette Aquino

188–189/272. Magdi Rodriguez

190–191/273. Candy Woolley

192–193/274. Jeannette Aquino

194–195/275. Thais Yanes

196/283. Robert Ramsay

PHOTO CREDITS
(Student Edition page/Teacher Edition page)

8/8. © www.corbis.com/CORBIS

50/55. Girl singing: © EyeWire Collection; Marimba players: © Dave G. Houser/CORBIS

108–109/145. Garth Brooks: © Nubar Alexanian/CORBIS; Candlelit Choir: ©Bob Krist/CORBIS; Rolling Stones: © Lynn Goldsmith/CORBIS

Fine Art Credits

The Sleeping Muse III, circa 1917 (marble). Constantin Brancusi (1876–1957). © 2003 Artists Rights Society (ARS), New York/ADAGP, Paris. Transparency: Private Collection/Christie's Images/Bridgeman Art Library.
    pg. 18 Student Edition   pg. 22 Teacher Edition

Whirligig, entitled "America," c.1938–42. Frank Memkus, American, 1895–1965. Wood and metal (height with paddle up): 80 3/4 x 29 x 40 in., Restricted gift of Marshall Field, Mr. and Mrs. Robert A. Kubiceck, Mr. James Raoul Simmons, Mrs. Esther Sparks, Mrs. Frank L. Sulzberger and the Oak Park–River Forest Associates of the Woman's Board of The Art Institute of Chicago, 1980.166. photo © The Art Institute of Chicago.
    pg. 30 Student Edition   pg. 33 Teacher Edition

Conversation, 1992. Bridget Riley. Oil on linen. 2002 © Bridget Riley, All Rights Reserved, Courtesy Karsten Schubert, London. Transparency: Reproduced by courtesy of Abbot Hall Art Gallery, Kendal, UK.
    pg. 42 Student Edition   pg. 47 Teacher Edition

Abstraction, Porch Shadows, Twin Lakes, Connecticut, 1916. Paul Strand. © 1971 Aperture Foundation Inc., Paul Strand Archive.
    pg. 43 Student Edition   pg. 47 Teacher Edition

Nine Lives from *In a Nutshell: Charlie the Red Cat* by Jim Tweedy © Jim Tweedy.
    pg. 68 Student Edition   pg. 80 Teacher Edition

Campbell's Tomato Juice. Andy Warhol (1928–1987). Sculpture, 1964. 6 boxes, synthetic polymer paint and silkscreen on wood. © 2002 Andy Warhol Foundation/ARS, NY/TM Licensed by Campbell's Soup Co. All Rights Reserved. © 2003 Andy Warhol Foundation for the Visual Arts/ARS, New York. Transparency: The Newark Museum, Newark, New Jersey, U.S.A. © The Newark Museum/Art Resource, NY.
    pg. 69 Student Edition   pg. 85 Teacher Edition

La Gare Sainte-Lazare, 1877. Claude Monet (1840–1926). (Oil on canvas.) Transparency: Photo: Herve Lewandowski. Musée d'Orsay, Paris, France. © Réunion des Musées Nationaux/Art Resource, NY.
    pg. 78 Student Edition   pg. 93 Teacher Edition

Montagne Sainte-Victoire (seen from Bibemus Quarry). Paul Cezanne (1839–1906). (Oil on canvas.) Transparency: The Barnes Foundation, Merion, Pennsylvania, USA/Bridgeman Art Library.
    pg. 88 Student Edition   pg. 103 Teacher Edition

Calico Bunny, 1997. Claes Oldenburg. Screenprint on sewn canvas, stuffed with polyester, painted wood, metal. 13 x 10 x 6 in. (33 x 25.5 x 15 cm). Edition of 99 (33 each in red, yellow, and blue). Published in part by The Fabric Workshop and Museum. Photo by Graydon Wood. Reproduced with permission of the artist.
    pg. 89 Student Edition   pg. 109 Teacher Edition

Yellow Band, Mark Rothko. 1956, oil on canvas. © 1998 Kate Rothko Prizel & Christopher Rothko/Artists Rights Society (ARS), New York. Transparency: Sheldon Memorial Art Gallery, University of Nebraska–Lincoln, NAA, Thomas C. Woods Memorial Collection.
    pg. 98 Student Edition   pg. 118 Teacher Edition

Autumn. Grandma Moses. The Bennington Museum, Bennington, Vermont © 1985, Grandma Moses Properties Co., New York.
    pg. 104 Student Edition   pg. 127 Teacher Edition

Miss Liberty by Edward Ambrose. Collection of Meadow Farm Museum, County of Henrico, Virginia. All Rights Reserved.
    pg. 105 Student Edition   pg. 128 Teacher Edition

Galloping Horse by Eadweard Muybridge (1830–1904). Plate 628 from "Animal Locomotion," 1887. Stapleton Collection, UK/Bridgeman Art Library.
    pg. 114 Student Edition   pg. 153 Teacher Edition

Tree with Dancing Figures. 1995. by Patrick Davis, Photograph by Alan Sprecher, Collection of the American Visionary Art Museum.
    pg. 118 Student Edition   pg. 159 Teacher Edition

Tracking Center. by Michele Hardy. Quilt. © Michele Hardy.
    pg. 120 Student Edition   pg. 167 Teacher Edition

Chichen Itza. by Robert Frerck. Photograph. © Robert Frerck/Woodfin Camp & Associates.
    pg. 134 Student Edition   pg. 179 Teacher Edition

Young Corn. Grant Wood, 1931. Oil on masonite panel, 23 1/2 x 29 7/8 inches. © Cedar Rapids, Iowa, Community School District, Memorial to Linnie Schloeman, Woodrow Wilson School.
    pg. 138 Student Edition   pg. 186 Teacher Edition

Dancer, c. 1918–1919. Elie Nadelman (1882–1946). Cherrywood (sculpture). Reproduced by permission of Elie Nadelman Estate. Gift in memory of Muriel Rand by her husband William Rand. The Jewish Museum, New York, N.Y., U.S.A. Transparency: © The Jewish Museum of New York/Art Recource, NY.
    pg. 154 Student Edition   pg. 210 Teacher Edition

Cuckoo Clock with squirrels and bird. #MD406–16. Used by permission of River City Cuckoo Clocks, La Crosse Instruments, La Crescent, MN
    pg. 185 Student Edition   pg. 254 Teacher Edition

Contents

SONGS AND CHANTS:

"Ambos a Dos" 122–123
"America" 24–25
"America, the Beautiful" 52–53
"Bate, Bate" (chant) 19
"Bingo" 4–5
"Cheki, Morena" 166–167
"Come and Sing" 56–57, 72–73
"Don Gato" 152–153
"Double Double Ice Ice" (chant) 38–39, 46–47
"El Gato y el Raton" 140–141
"El Juego Chirimbolo" 112–113, 116–117
"Get on Board" 74–75
"Going Over the Sea" 178–179
"Goodbye Song" 10–11
"Haak Gyo Jong" 64–65
"Hao Peng You" 126–127
"Hello Song" 14–15
"Hunt the Cows" 66–67
"Jump Jim Joe" 32–33, 194–195
"Lady, Lady" 12
"Li'l Liza Jane" 96–97
"Make New Friends" 2
"The Marvelous Toy" 124–125
"The Noble Duke of York" 130–131
"O, Susanna" 100–101
"Oats, Peas, Beans" 136–137
"Penny Song" 162–163
"Polly Wolly Doodle" 80–81
"Sally Go 'Round the Sun" 168–169
"Saute, Crapaud!" 160–161
"Shoo, Fly" 48–49, 190–191
"Skip to My Lou" 60–61
"Spanish Zoo Rhythms" (chant) 148–149
"Suo Gan" 16–17
"Ten in the Bed" 84–85
"This Old Man" 20–21, 44–45
"Tinga Layo" 92–93
"Yankee Doodle" 28–29
"You're a Grand Old Flag" 26–27
"Yum, Yum" (chant) 40–41

ARTIST PORTRAITS:

Ray Charles 8
Gloria Estefan 106–107
Zoltán Kodály .184

GAMES:

"Name Game" 3
"Jump Jim Joe" 34–35
"Penny Song" 162–163

FINE ART:

Abstraction, Porch Shadows, Twin Lakes, Connecticut, 1916 by Paul Strand 43
Autumn by Grandma Moses 104
Calico Bunny by Claes Oldenburg 89
Campbell's Tomato Juice by Andy Warhol 69
Chichen Itza by Robert Frerck 134
Conversation by Bridget Riley 42
Cuckoo Clock with Squirrels and bird 185
Dancer by Elie Nadelman 154
Galloping Horse by Eadweard Muybridge 114
La Gare Saint-Lazare by Claude Monet 78
Miss Liberty by Edward Ambrose 105
Montagne Sainte-Victoire (seen from Bibemus Quarry) by Paul Cezanne 88
Nine Lives by Jim Tweedy 68
The Sleeping Muse III by Constantin Brancusi 18
Tracking Center by Michele Hardy 120
Tree with Dancing Figures by Patrick Davis 118
Whirligig, entitled "America" by Frank Memkus 30
Yellow Band by Mark Rothko 98
Young Corn by Grant Wood 138

Maestro

Make New Friends

TRADITIONAL FRIENDSHIP SONG
Arranged by MICHAEL STORY

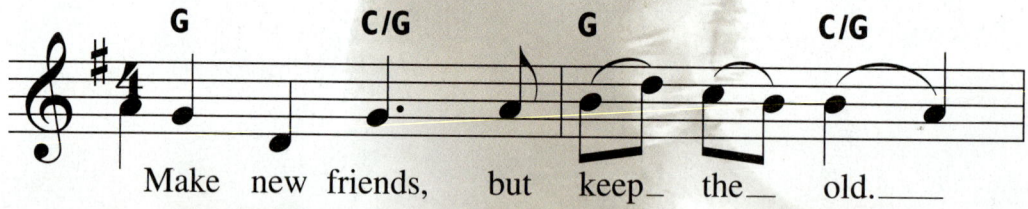

Make new friends, but keep the old.

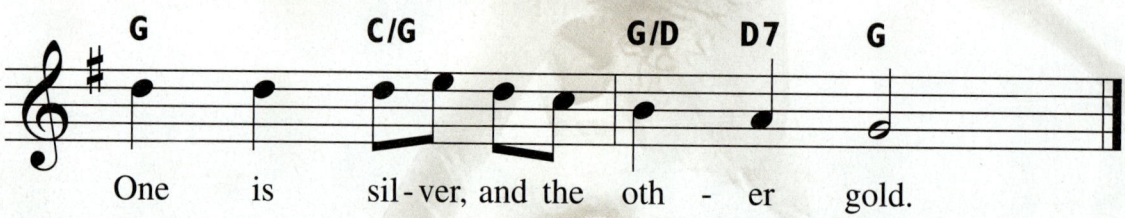

One is sil-ver, and the oth-er gold.

© 2003 BEAM ME UP MUSIC (ASCAP)   All Rights Administered by WARNER BROS. PUBLICATIONS U.S. INC.   All Rights Reserved

NAME GAME

ECHO=REPEAT OR COPY

Oliver
Marisa
Alexa
Brigitta
Maria
Sven
Bryan
Katie
Mai

BINGO

AMERICAN GAME SONG
Arranged by MICHAEL STORY

There was a farm-er had a dog, and

Bin - go was his name - o.   B - I - N - G - O,
(clap) - I - N - G - O,
(clap,   clap) - N - G - O,
(clap,   clap,   clap) - G - O,
(clap,   clap,   clap, clap) - O,
(clap,   clap,   clap, clap, clap)

B - I - N - G - O,   B - I - N - G - O, and
(clap) - I - N - G - O,   (clap) - I - N - G - O, and
(clap, clap) - N - G - O,   (clap, clap) - N - G - O, and
(clap, clap, clap) - G - O,   (clap, clap, clap) - G - O, and
(clap, clap, clap, clap) - O,   (clap, clap, clap, clap) - O, and
(clap, clap, clap, clap, clap)   (clap, clap, clap, clap, clap) and

Bin - go was his name - o. There

© 2003 BEAM ME UP MUSIC (ASCAP)   All Rights Administered by WARNER BROS. PUBLICATIONS U.S. INC.   All Rights Reserved

Ray Charles

Goodbye Song

By ART WILLIAMS
and ROBERT W. SMITH
Arranged by ROBERT W. SMITH

Good - bye. Good - bye, to you and all our friends. Good-

bye. Good - bye, our time's come to an end. Good -

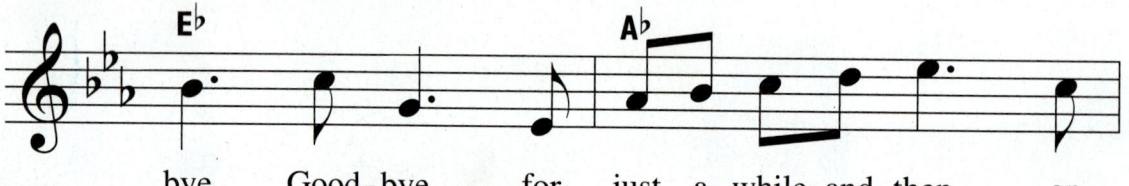

bye. Good - bye, for just a while and then, an -

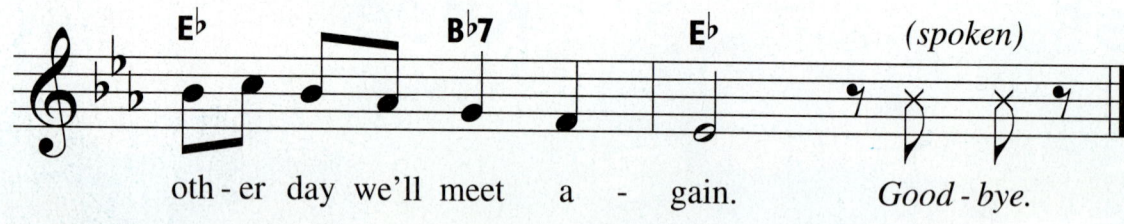

oth - er day we'll meet a - gain. *Good - bye.*

© 2003 BEAM ME UP MUSIC (ASCAP)   All Rights Administered by WARNER BROS. PUBLICATIONS U.S. INC.   All Rights Reserved

Lady, Lady

Adapted and Arranged by
ROBERT W. SMITH

La - dy, la - dy,

buy a broom for my ba - by.

Sweep it low, sweep it high, sweep the cob - webs

out of the sky. La - dy, la - dy,

buy a broom for my ba - by.

© 2003 BEAM ME UP MUSIC (ASCAP)   All Rights Administered by WARNER BROS. PUBLICATIONS U.S. INC.   All Rights Reserved

photo credit: Donald Norsworthy

HELLO SONG

By ART WILLIAMS
and ROBERT W. SMITH
Arranged by ROBERT W. SMITH

Happily!

Hel - lo. Hel - lo, and how are you to-day?_ Hel-

lo. Hel - lo, I'm glad you came my way. Hel -
(We're) (our)

lo. Hel - lo, I hope you're here to stay. It's
(We)

friends like you that make my day. *Hel - lo!*
(our)

© 2003 BEAM ME UP MUSIC (ASCAP)   All Rights Administered by WARNER BROS. PUBLICATIONS U.S. INC.   All Rights Reserved

Suo Gan

WELSH LULLABY
Arranged by ROBERT W. SMITH

Su - o gan, do not weep, su - o gan, go to sleep.

Su - o gan, Moth-er's near, su - o gan, have no fear.

Su - o gan, do not weep, su - o gan, go to sleep.

Su - o gan, Moth-er's near, su - o gan, have no fear.

© 2003 BEAM ME UP MUSIC (ASCAP)   All Rights Administered by WARNER BROS. PUBLICATIONS U.S. INC.   All Rights Reserved

Map of England & Wales

Scotland

Irish Sea

Wales

England

The English Channel

The Sleeping Muse III by Constantin Brancusi

Uno   dos   tres   **cho-**

Uno   dos   tres   **co-**

Uno   dos   tres   **la-**

Uno   dos   tres   **te**

America

TRADITIONAL ENGLISH MELODY
Words by SAMUEL FRANCIS SMITH
Arranged by MICHAEL STORY

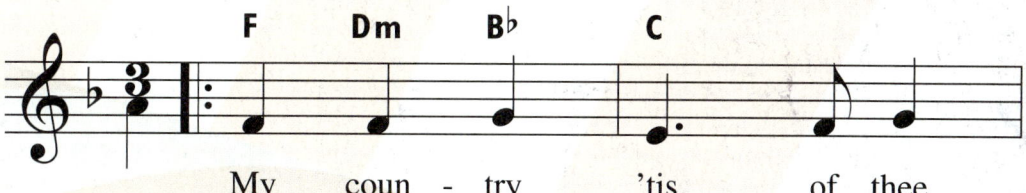

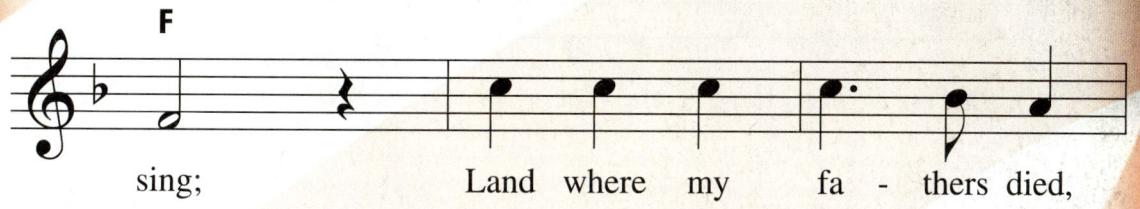

© 2003 BEAM ME UP MUSIC (ASCAP)   All Rights Administered by WARNER BROS. PUBLICATIONS U.S. INC.   All Rights Reserved

You're a Grand Old Flag

By GEORGE M. COHAN
Arranged by MICHAEL STORY

You're a grand old flag, you're a high fly-ing flag; and for-ev-er in peace may you wave;_____ you're the em-blem of the land I love, the home of the free and the

© 2003 BEAM ME UP MUSIC (ASCAP)   All Rights Administered by WARNER BROS. PUBLICATIONS U.S. INC.   All Rights Reserved

Whirligig, entitled "America" by Frank Memkus

Me and

My Shadow

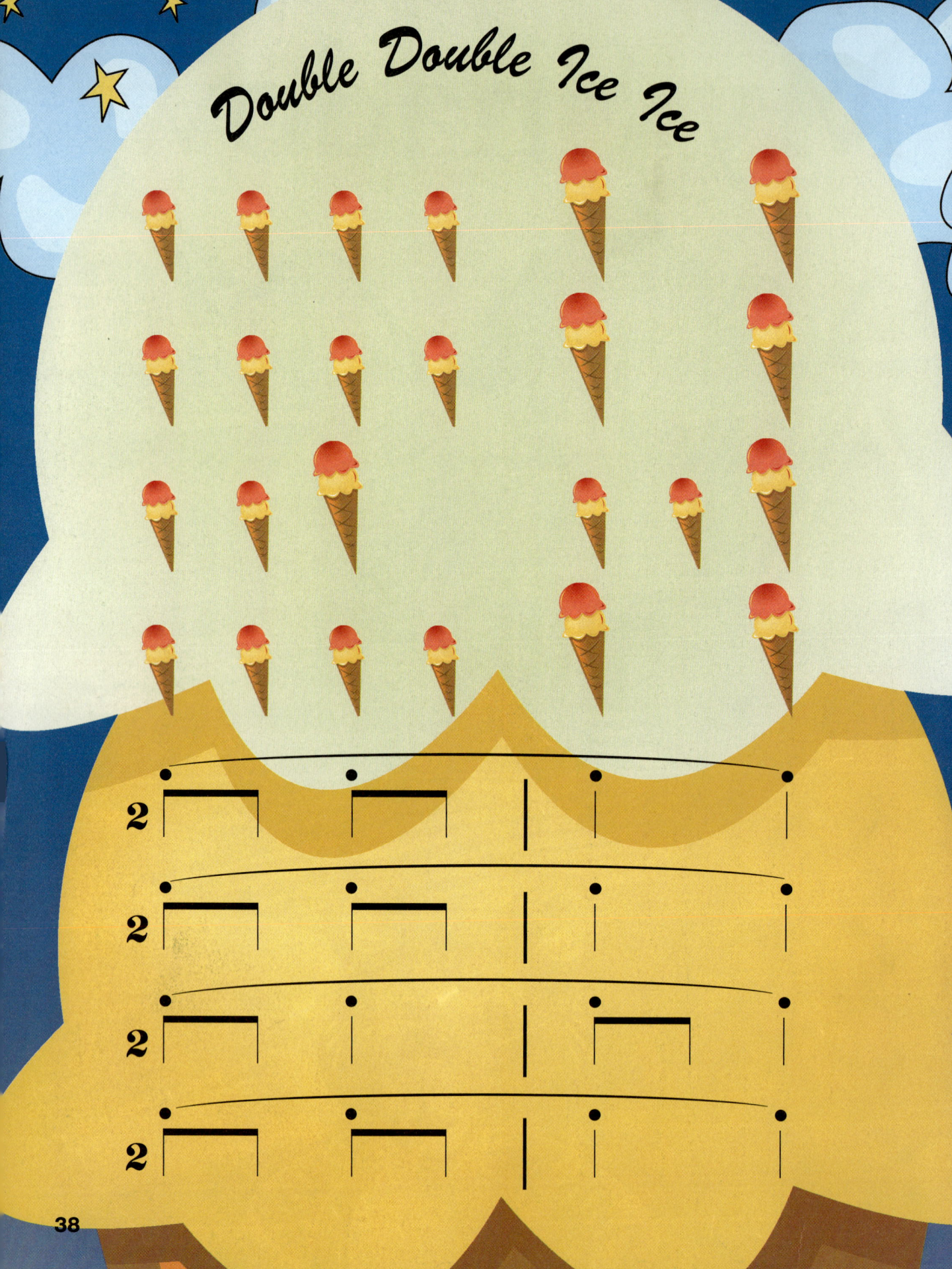

Conversation by Bridget Riley

Abstraction, Porch Shadows, Twin Lakes, Connecticut, 1916 by Paul Strand

This Old Man

E♭ F7 B♭ B♭7
shed His grace on thee. And
E♭(2) B♭
crown thy good with broth - er - hood, from
E♭ F7 B♭
sea to shin - ing sea.

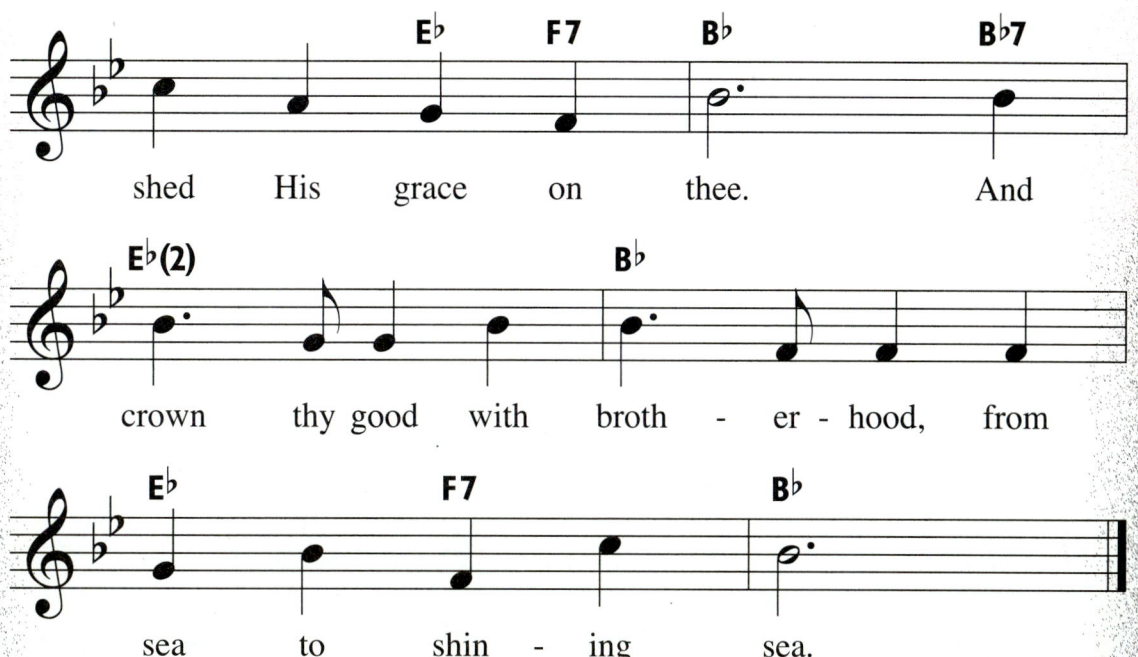

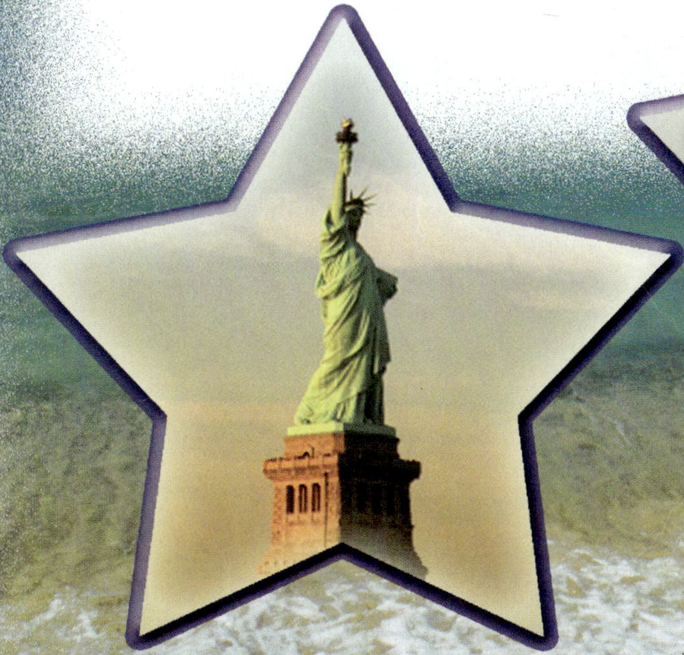

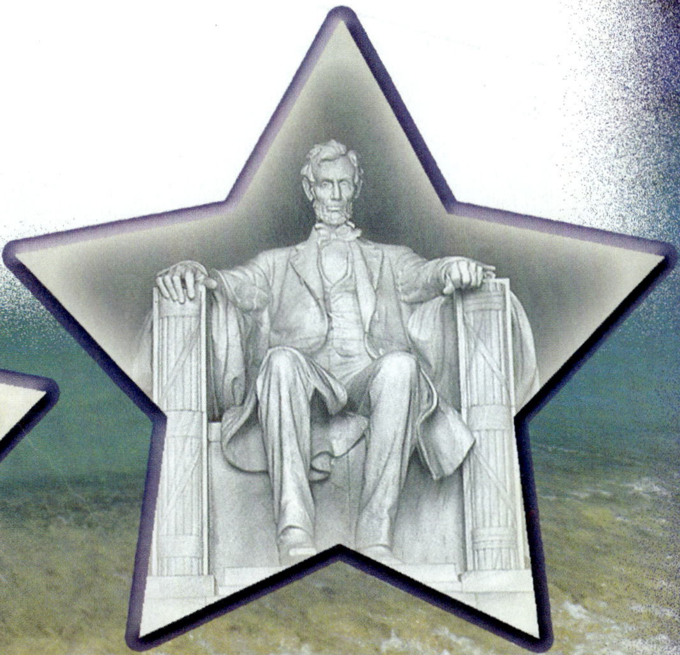

America,

the Beautiful

Play 4 times

1. **3** 𝄆 | 𝄽 𝄽 | | 𝄽 𝄽 | 𝄇

Play 4 times

2. **3** 𝄆 𝄽 | | | 𝄽 | | | 𝄇

Play 4 times

3. **3** 𝄆 ♩ | | ♩ | | 𝄇

     do   sol do   sol

Come and Sing

Adapted and Arranged by
MICHAEL STORY

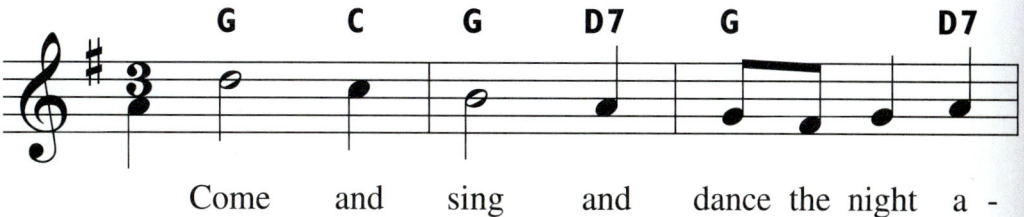

Come and sing and dance the night a-

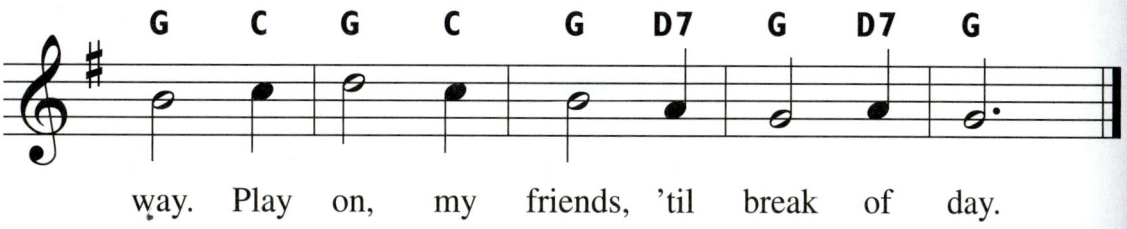

way. Play on, my friends, 'til break of day.

© 2003 BEAM ME UP MUSIC (ASCAP)   All Rights Administered by WARNER BROS. PUBLICATIONS U.S. INC.   All Rights Reserved

Choose the phrase:

1.
2.

How many beats are in each phrase?

Hunt the Cows

TRADITIONAL SINGING GAME
Arranged by ROBERT W. SMITH

A Brightly

Wake up you sleep-y head and go and get the cat-tle,
wake up you sleep-y head and go and get the cows.

B Slowly, as if tired

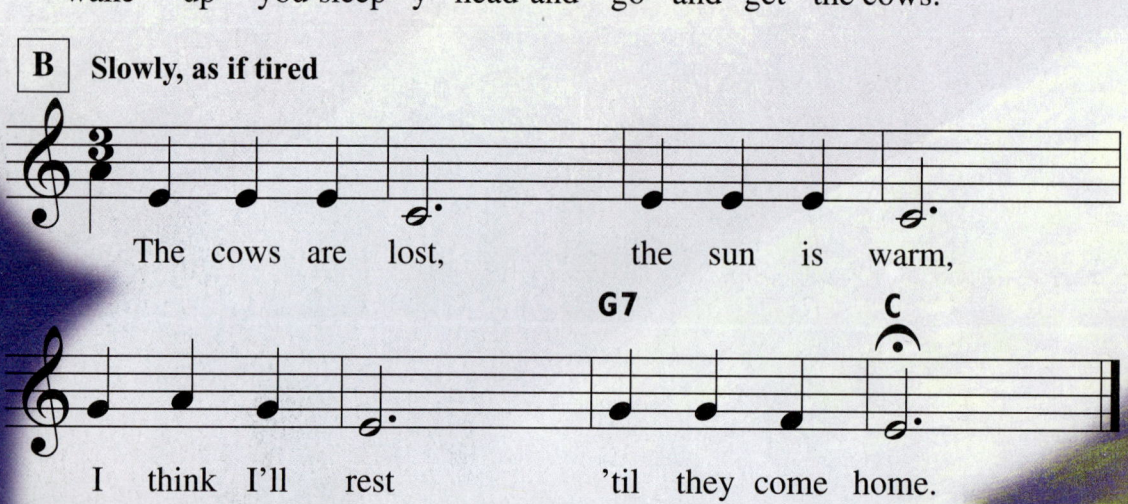

The cows are lost, the sun is warm,
I think I'll rest 'til they come home.

© 2003 BEAM ME UP MUSIC (ASCAP)   All Rights Administered by WARNER BROS. PUBLICATIONS U.S. INC.   All Rights Reserved

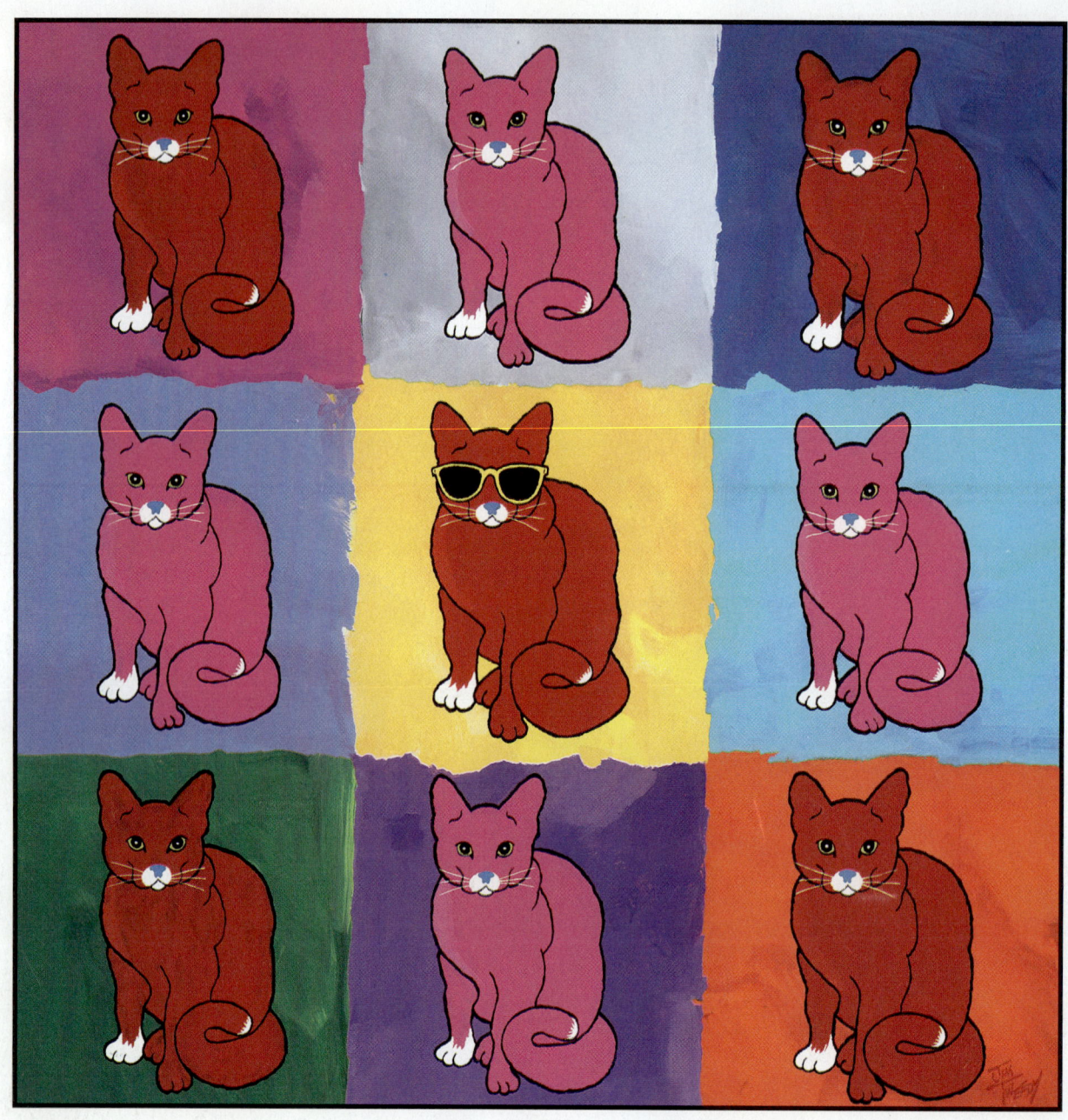

Nine Lives by Jim Tweedy

Campbell's Tomato Juice by Andy Warhol

PATTERNS REPEAT

Chant:

Pat - terns re - peat.

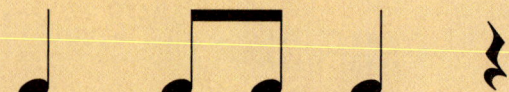
Pat - terns re - peat.

Put them in our hands and then in our feet.

Rhythm Patterns:

clap…

stomp…

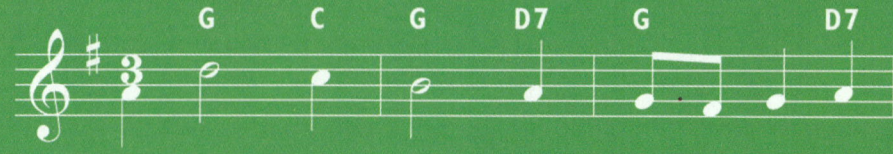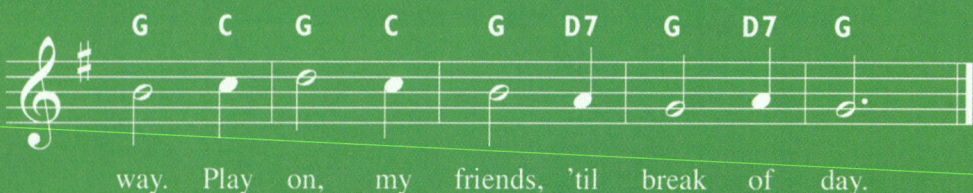

Repeated Tones

La Gare Sainte-Lazare by Claude Monet

Polly Wolly Doodle

SOUTHERN UNITED STATES
Arranged by JACK BULLOCK

Verse:

1. Oh, I went down south for to see my Sal, sing-ing Pol-ly Wol-ly Doo-dle all the day. My Sal-ly she's a spunk-y gal, sing Pol-ly Wol-ly Doo-dle all the

Sal, she is a maid-en fair, sing-ing Pol-ly Wol-ly Doo-dle all the day. With curl-y eyes and laugh-ing hair, sing Pol-ly Wol-ly Doo-dle all the

© 2003 BEAM ME UP MUSIC (ASCAP)   All Rights Administered by WARNER BROS. PUBLICATIONS U.S. INC.   All Rights Reserved

Ten in the Bed

Adapted and Arranged by
MICHAEL STORY

1. There were ten in the bed, and the
   nine…
   eight…
   seven…
   six…
   five…
   four…
   three…
   two…

lit-tle one said, "Roll o - ver! *sol mi do* Roll o - ver!" So they

all rolled o - ver and one fell out... 2.–9. There were

Last time

10. There was one in the bed, and the

Slowly

lit-tle one said, "Good night."

© 2003 BEAM ME UP MUSIC (ASCAP) All Rights Administered by WARNER BROS. PUBLICATIONS U.S. INC. All Rights Reserved

Montagne Sainte-Victoire (seen from Bibemus Quarry) by Paul Cezanne

Calico Bunny by Claes Oldenburg

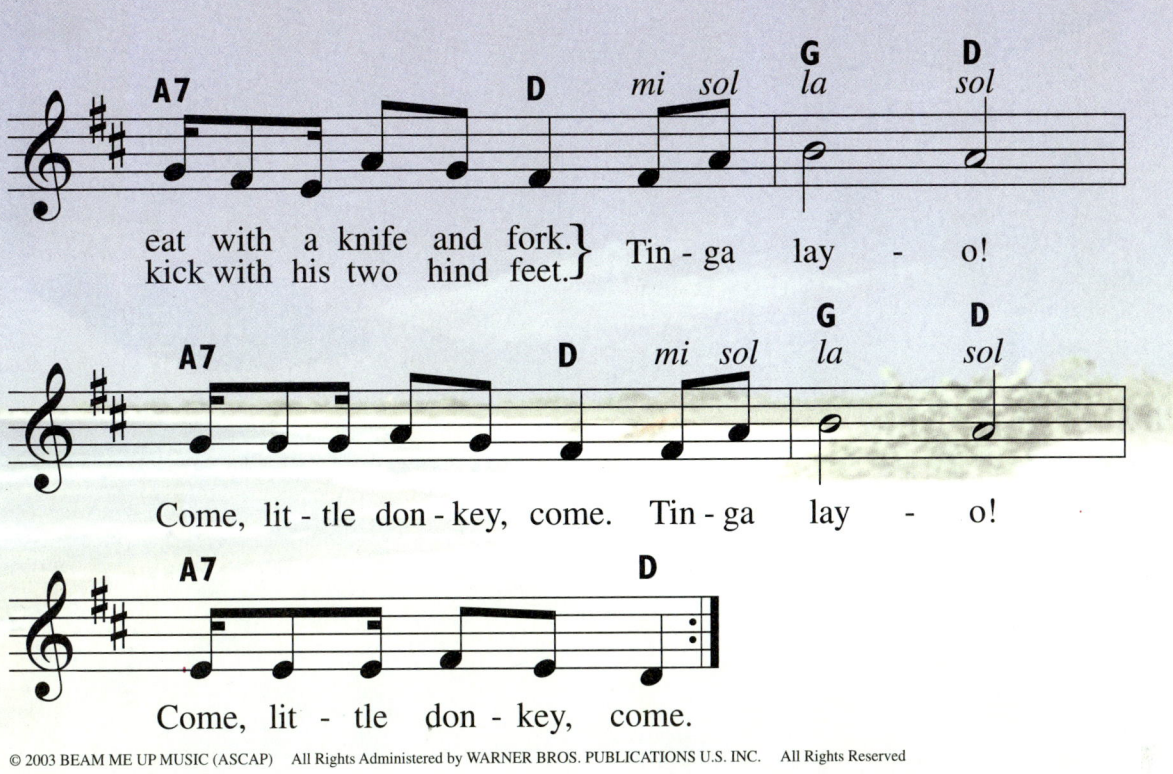
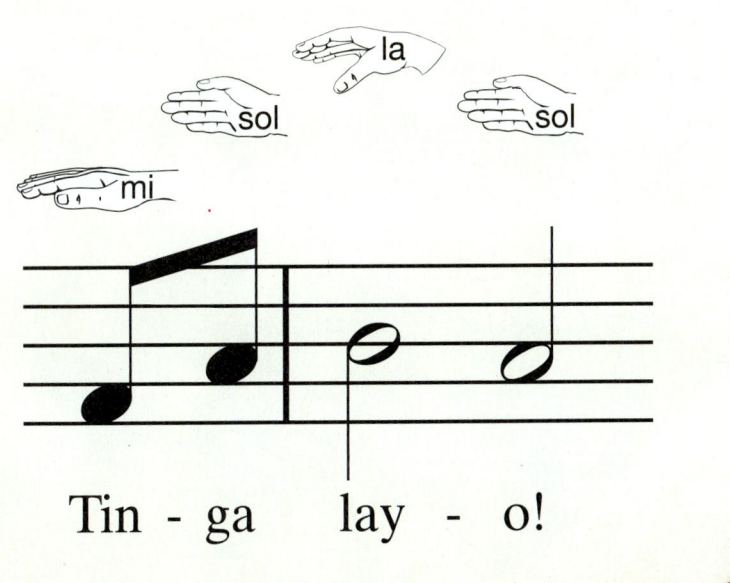

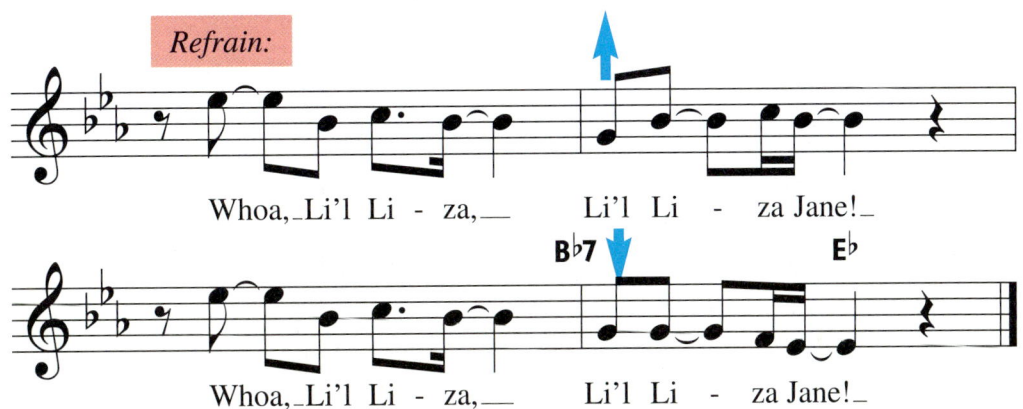

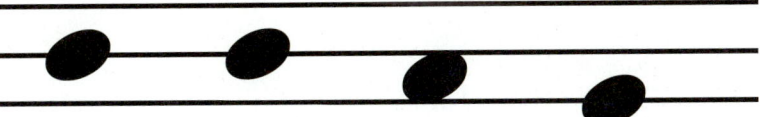
Find the arrows that point upward and downward. Listen! Which melody patterns go downward?

Yellow Band by Mark Rothko

Rhythm Groove

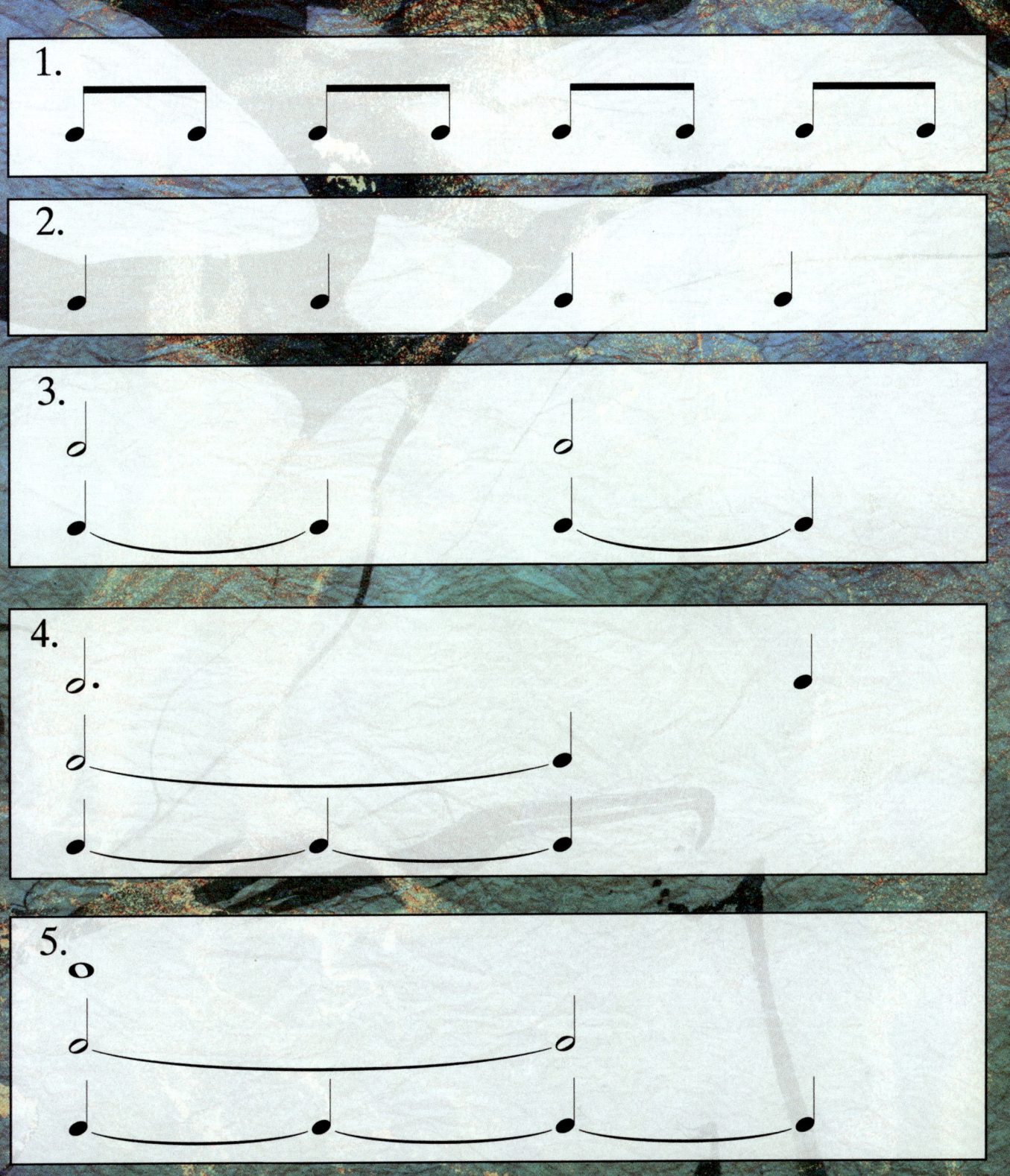

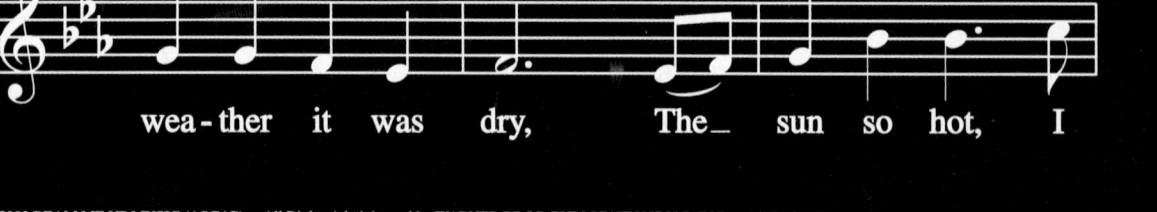

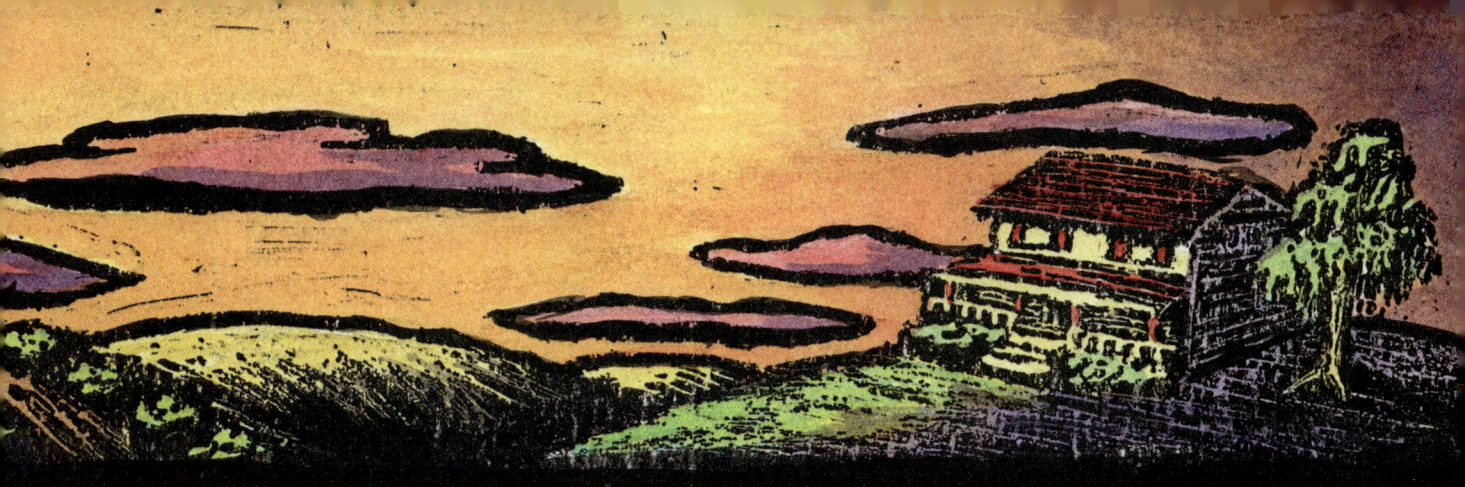

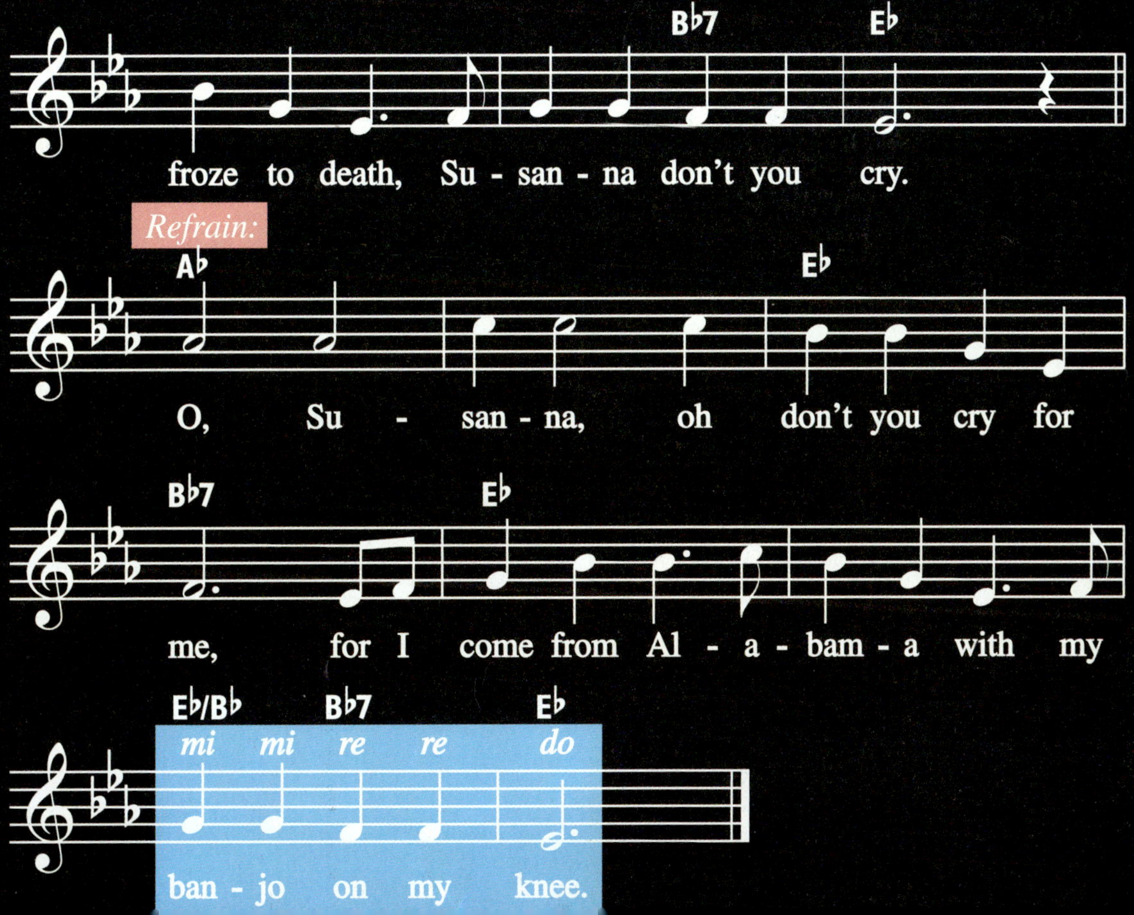
B♭7 E♭
froze to death, Su - san - na don't you cry.
Refrain:
A♭ E♭
O, Su - san - na, oh don't you cry for
B♭7 E♭
me, for I come from Al - a - bam - a with my
E♭/B♭ B♭7 E♭
mi mi re re do
ban - jo on my knee.

Miss Liberty by Edward Ambrose

Autumn by Grandma Moses

GLORIA ESTEFAN

Photo: Maggie Rodriguez

Photo: Larry Busacca

Photo: Neal Preston

Photo: David Bergman

108

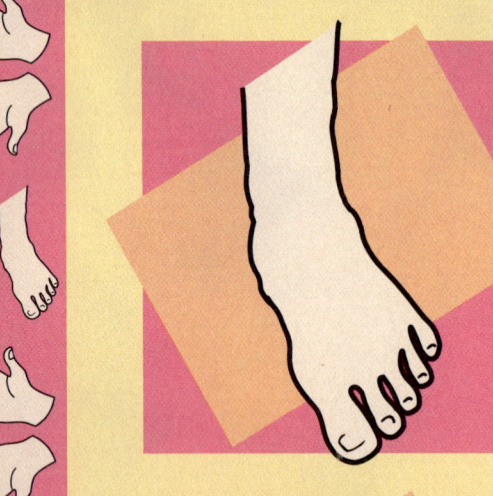

Pie
Foot

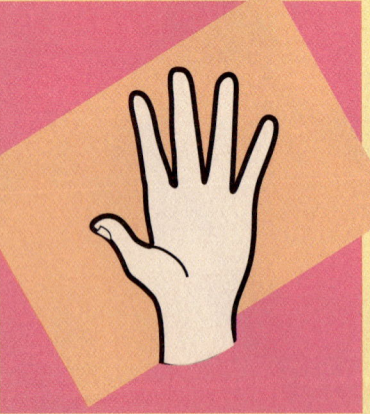

Mano
Hand

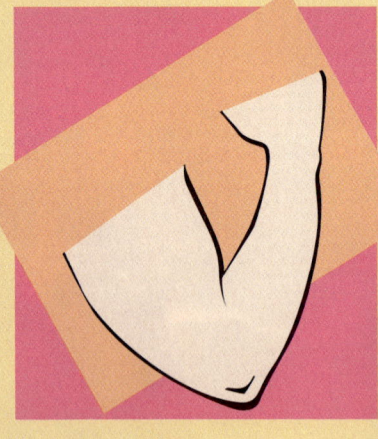

Codo
Elbow

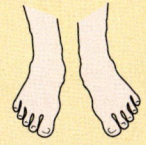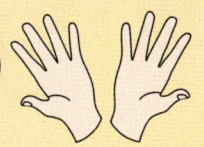

El Juego Chirimbolo

(The Thingamajig Game)

Adapted and Arranged by
VICTOR LOPEZ

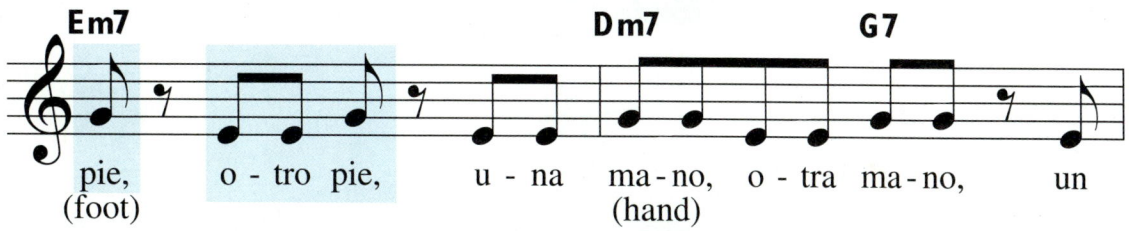

© 2003 BEAM ME UP MUSIC (ASCAP)   All Rights Administered by WARNER BROS. PUBLICATIONS U.S. INC.   All Rights Reserved

Galloping Horse, plate 628 from "Animal Locomotion,"
1887 by Eadweard Muybridge

Match the Animal With Its Rhythm

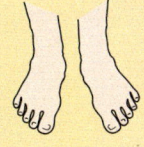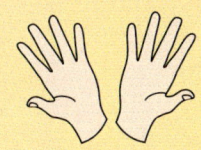

El Juego Chirimbolo

(The Thingamajig Game)

Adapted and Arranged by
VICTOR LOPEZ

El jue-go chi-rim-bo-lo que bo-ni-to es, con un pie, (foot) o-tro pie, u-na ma-no, o-tra ma-no, un (hand) co-do, o-tro co-do. (elbow) El jue-go chi-rim-bo-lo que bo-ni-to es, con un pie, o-tro pie, u-na ma-no, o-tra ma-no, un co-do, o-tro co-do. El jue-go chi-rim-bo-lo que bo-ni-to es. *Play!*

© 2003 BEAM ME UP MUSIC (ASCAP)   All Rights Administered by WARNER BROS. PUBLICATIONS U.S. INC.   All Rights Reserved

Tree with Dancing Figures by Patrick Davis

Tracking Center by Michele Hardy

RONDO ALLA TURCA

Wolfgang Amadeus Mozart
From *Piano Sonata in A Major, K. 331*

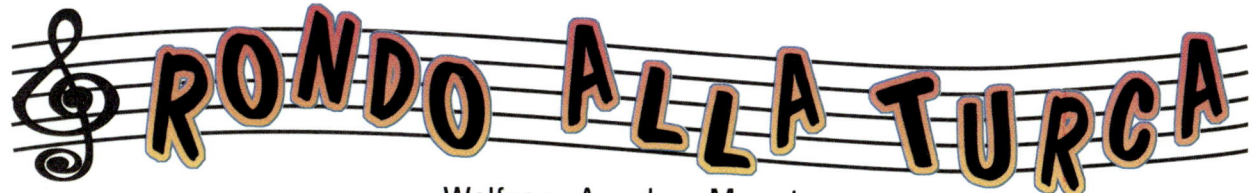

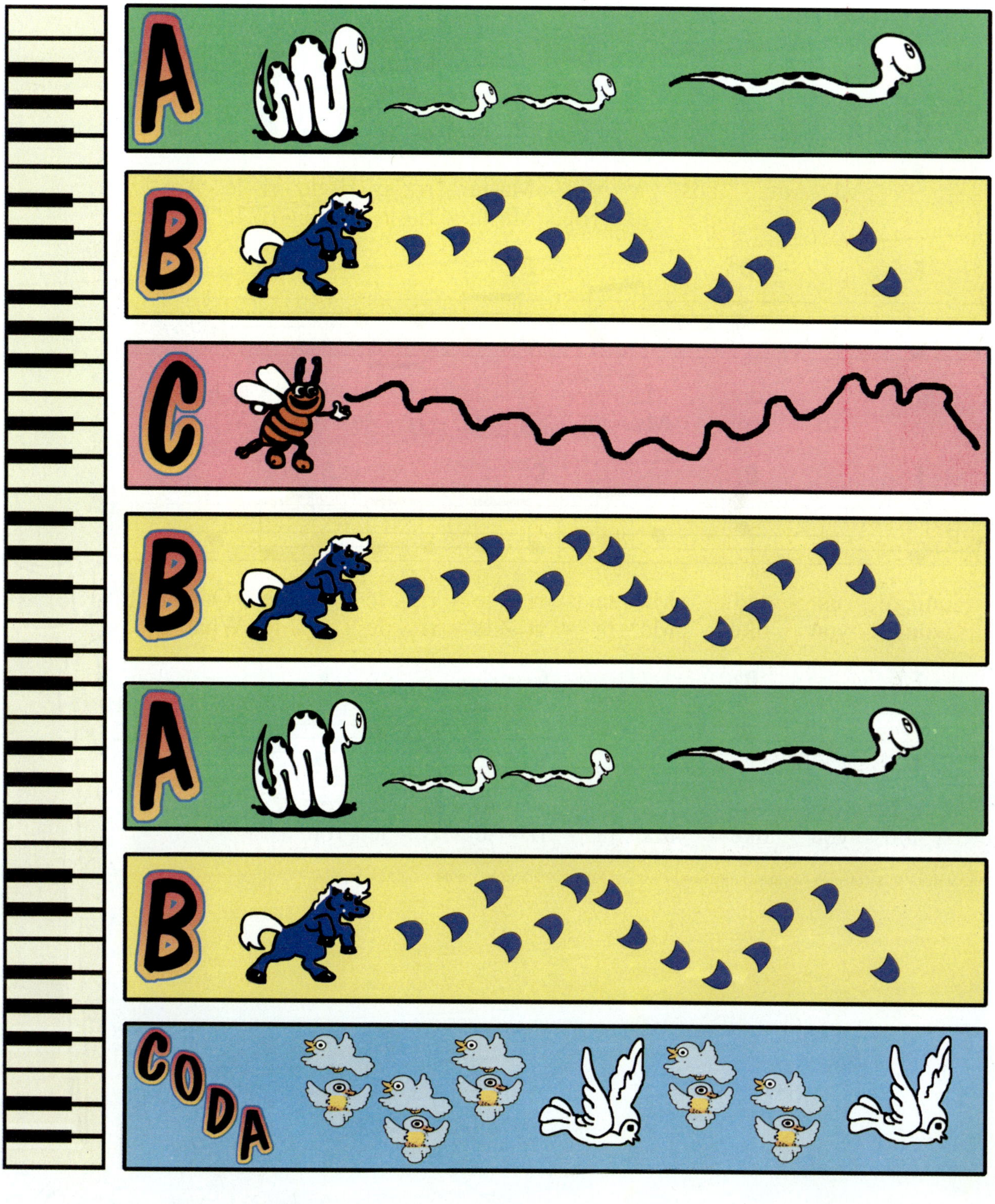

Ambos a Dos

PUERTO RICAN FOLK SONG
Arranged by VICTOR LOPEZ

1. Am - bos a dos, Ma - ta - ri - le - ri - le - ri - le. Am-
   me to you, Ma - ta - ri - le - ri - le - ri - le. From

bos a dos, Ma - ta - ri - le - ri - le - rón. ¿Qué
me to you, Ma - ta - ri - le - ri - le - rón. What

quiere us - ted? Ma - ta - ri - le - ri - le - ri - le. ¿Qué
would you like? Ma - ta - ri - le - ri - le - ri - le. What

quiere us - ted? Ma - ta - ri - le - ri - le - rón. 2. From
would you like? Ma - ta - ri - le - ri - le - rón.

© 2003 BEAM ME UP MUSIC (ASCAP)   All Rights Administered by WARNER BROS. PUBLICATIONS U.S. INC.   All Rights Reserved

THE MARVELOUS TOY

Words and Music by
TOM PAXTON

Refrain:

It went "zip" when it moved and "bop" when it stopped, "whirrr" when it stood still. I never knew just what it was, and I guess I never will.

© 1961, Renewed 1989 Cherry Lane Music Publishing Company, Inc./DreamWorks Songs
Worldwide Rights for DreamWorks Songs Administered by Cherry Lane Music Publishing Company, Inc.
All Rights Reserved   Used by Permission

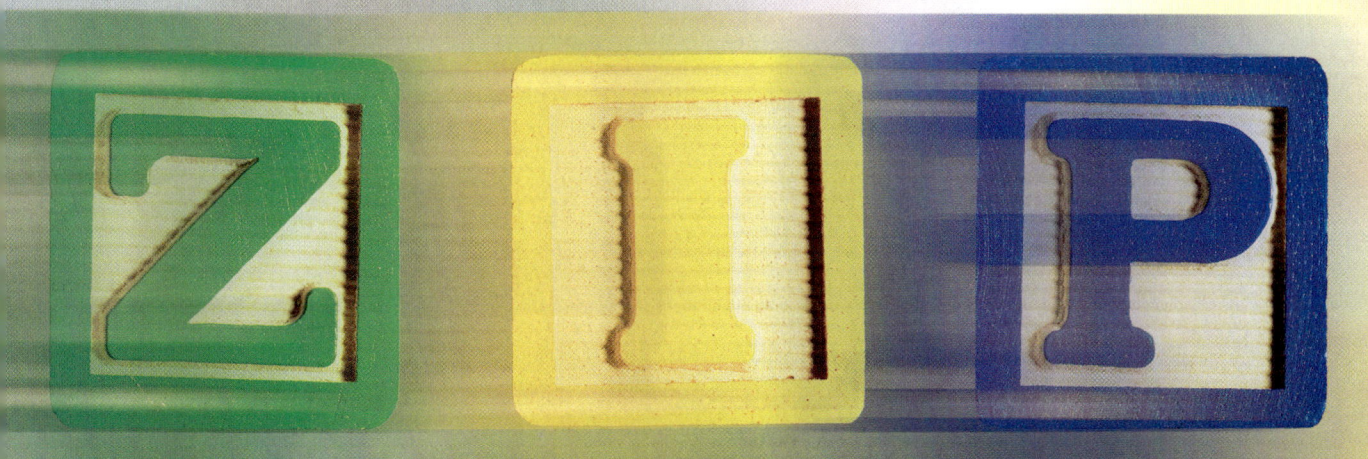

It went "zip"

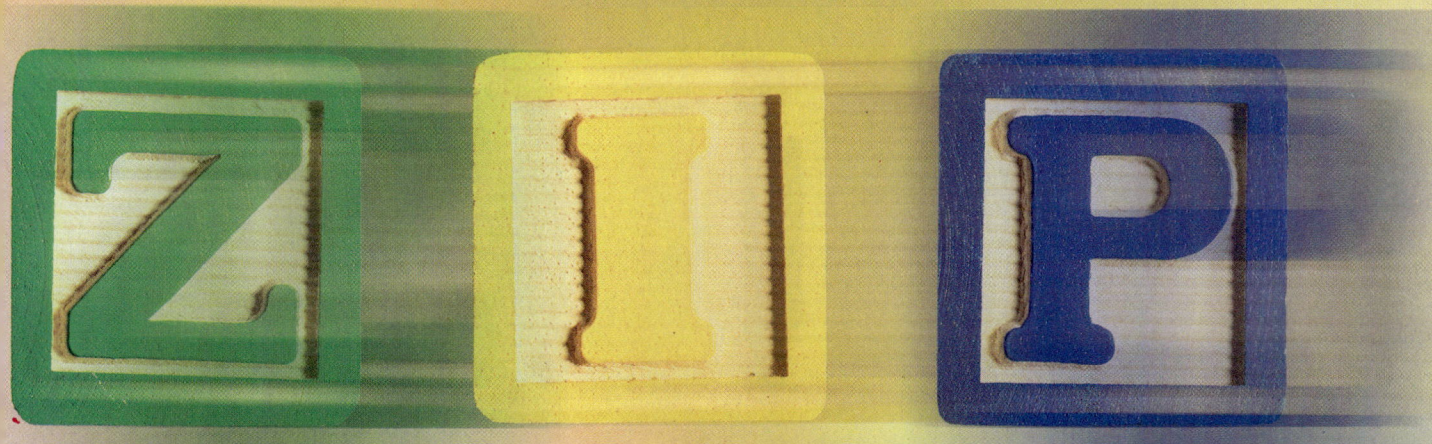

Hao Peng You

(Looking for a Friend)

CHINESE CHILDREN'S SONG
Arranged by ROBERT W. SMITH
Chinese Lyrics by MIN XIE SHAHEEN

Zhao ya, zhao ya, zhao ya, zhao,

Zhao dao yi ge hao peng you,

Jing ge li ya, jü ge gong, Xiao xi xi ya,

wo wo shou, Da jia yi qi ti-ao wu.

Ni shi wo di hao peng you. Zai jian!

English Translation:
Looking, looking, looking, looking,
I have found a good friend.
Salute, bow,
Smile, and shake hands.
Let's dance together, together.
You are my good friend.
Good-bye!

© 2003 BEAM ME UP MUSIC (ASCAP)   All Rights Administered by WARNER BROS. PUBLICATIONS U.S. INC.   All Rights Reserved

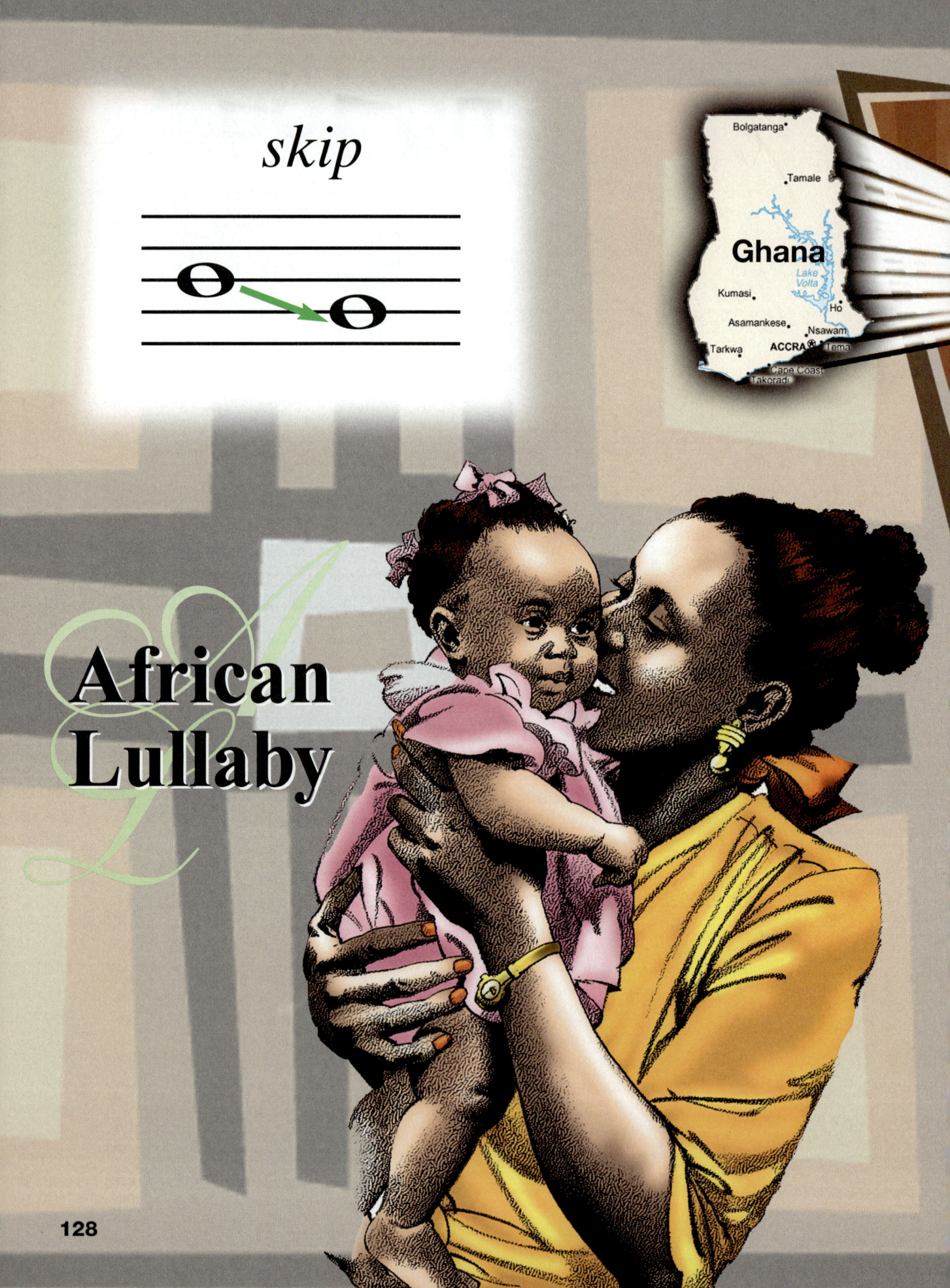

steps

The Noble Duke of York

TRADITIONAL ENGLISH
Arranged by MICHAEL STORY

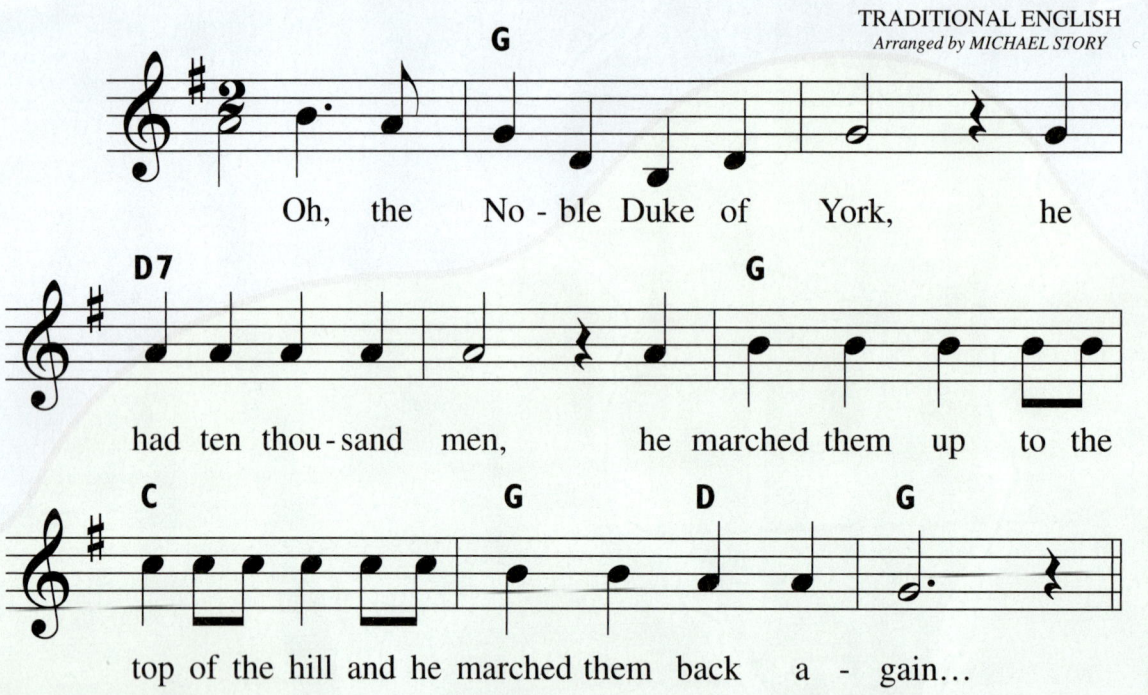

Oh, the No-ble Duke of York, he had ten thou-sand men, he marched them up to the top of the hill and he marched them back a - gain...

© 2003 BEAM ME UP MUSIC (ASCAP)   All Rights Administered by WARNER BROS. PUBLICATIONS U.S. INC.   All Rights Reserved

Chichen Itza by Robert Frerck

Young Corn by Grant Wood

El Gato y el Ratón

(The Cat and the Mouse)

SPANISH SONG
Arranged by VICTOR LOPEZ

El Gato y el Ratón

(The Cat and the Mouse)

SPANISH SONG
Arranged by VICTOR LOPEZ

do do do re mi mi
Oh ga - ti - to, oh ga - ti - to, you will

mi mi re re do
nev - er cap - ture me...

© 2003 BEAM ME UP MUSIC (ASCAP)   All Rights Administered by WARNER BROS. PUBLICATIONS U.S. INC.   All Rights Reserved

United States of America

North Atlantic Ocean

Gulf of Mexico

Caribbean

Caribbean Sea

Central America

Panama

Pacific Ocean

South America

Spanish Zoo Rhythms

Choo-ee

Ratoncito

Qui-qui-ri-qui

Gallo

Miau, miau, miau ♫ ♩

Gato

Crr - - - oak ♩

Sapo

Spanish Zoo Music

Don Gato

MEXICAN FOLK SONG
Adapted and Arranged by ROBERT W. SMITH

1. Oh Señor Don Ga- to
   dore you," wrote the

2.3. *See extra lyrics*

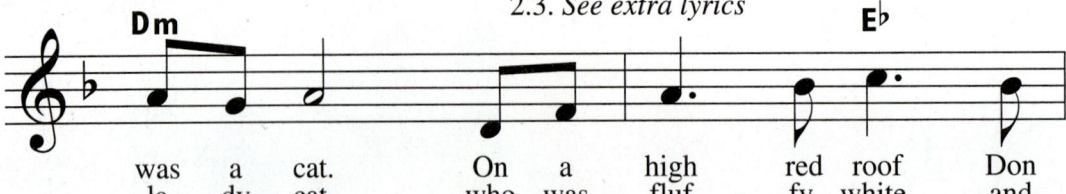

was a cat. On a high red roof Don
la- dy cat, who was fluf- fy, white, and

Ga- to sat. He went there to read a let- ter, meow, meow,
wore a hat. There was not a sweet- er kit- ty, meow, meow,

meow, where the read- ing light was bet- ter, meow, meow, meow. 'Twas a
meow, in the coun- try or the cit- y, meow, meow, meow, and she

love note for Don Ga- to._____ "I a-
said she'd wed Don Ga- to._____

Extra Lyrics:

2. Oh Don Gato jumped so happily.
   He fell off the roof and broke his knee.
   Broke his ribs and all his whiskers,
   Meow, meow, meow,
   And his little solar plexus,
   Meow, meow, meow.
   "Ay carumba," cried Don Gato.
   Then the doctors all came on the run,
   Just to see if something could be done.
   And they held a consultation,
   Meow, meow, meow,
   About how to save their patient,
   Meow, meow, meow,
   "Can we save Señor Don Gato?"

3. But in spite of ev'rything they tried,
   Poor Señor Don Gato up and died.
   And it wasn't very merry,
   Meow, meow, meow,
   Going to the cemetery,
   Meow, meow, meow.
   For the ending of Don Gato.
   When the fun'ral passed the market square,
   Such a smell of fish was in the air.
   Though his burial was slated,
   Meow, meow, meow,
   He became reanimated,
   Meow, meow, meow.
   He came back to life, Don Gato.
   He came back to life, Don Gato!

© 2003 BEAM ME UP MUSIC (ASCAP)   All Rights Administered by WARNER BROS. PUBLICATIONS U.S. INC.   All Rights Reserved

Dancer by Elie Nadelman

Saute, Crapaud!
(Jump Up, Frog!)

CAJUN FOLK SONG
Translation by EMMA PERENNES

Saute, cra-paud, ta queue va brû-ler, prends donc cour-age, elle va re-pous-ser.

English Translation:
Jump up, frog, your tail is going to burn,
Just be brave, another will grow.

© 2003 BEAM ME UP MUSIC (ASCAP)   All Rights Administered by WARNER BROS. PUBLICATIONS U.S. INC.   All Rights Reserved

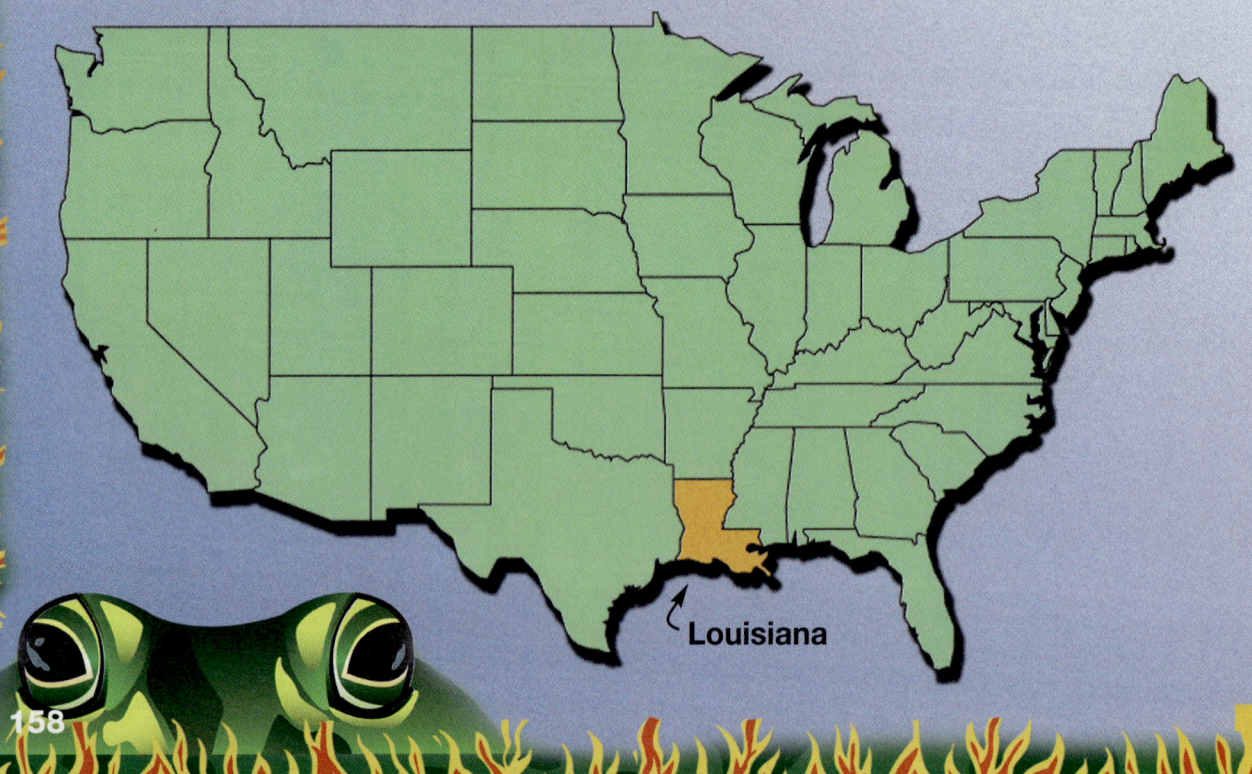

Penny Song

Adapted and Arranged by
JACK BULLOCK

There's a penny in my hand. It will trav-el through the land. Is it here? Is it there? It will trav-el ev-'ry-where.

Mar-y, do you have my pen-ny? No, I don't have your pen-ny. Bob, do you have my pen-ny? Yes, I do have your pen-ny.

© 2003 BEAM ME UP MUSIC (ASCAP)   All Rights Administered by WARNER BROS. PUBLICATIONS U.S. INC.   All Rights Reserved

Cheki, Morena
(Shake It!)

PUERTO RICAN GAME SONG

© 2003 BEAM ME UP MUSIC (ASCAP)   All Rights Administered by WARNER BROS. PUBLICATIONS U.S. INC.   All Rights Reserved

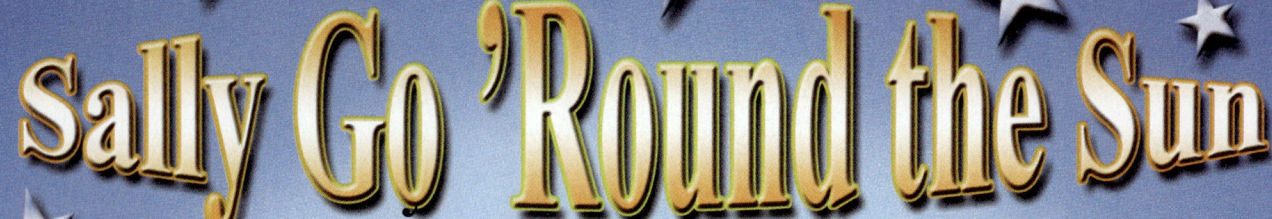

Sally Go 'Round the Sun

AMERICAN FOLK SONG
Arranged by MICHAEL STORY

Sal - ly go 'round the sun,

Sal - ly go 'round the moon,

Sal - ly go 'round the chim - ney pot

ev - 'ry af - ter - noon.

© 2003 BEAM ME UP MUSIC (ASCAP) All Rights Administered by WARNER BROS. PUBLICATIONS U.S. INC. All Rights Reserved

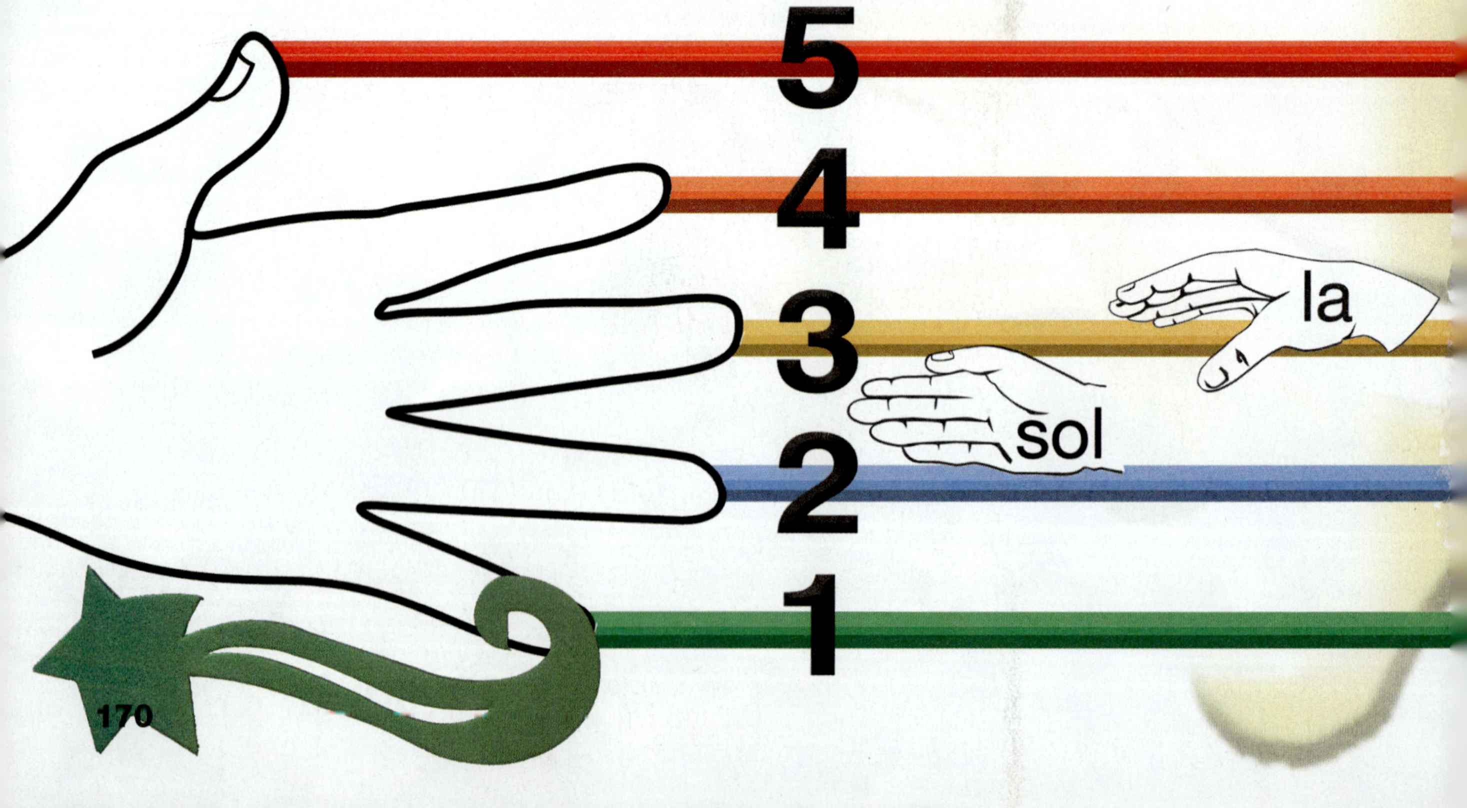

Sally Go 'Round the Sun

Sal - ly go 'round the sun,

Sal - ly go 'round the moon,

Sal-ly go 'round the chim-ney pot, ev-'ry af-ter-noon.

A-Courting

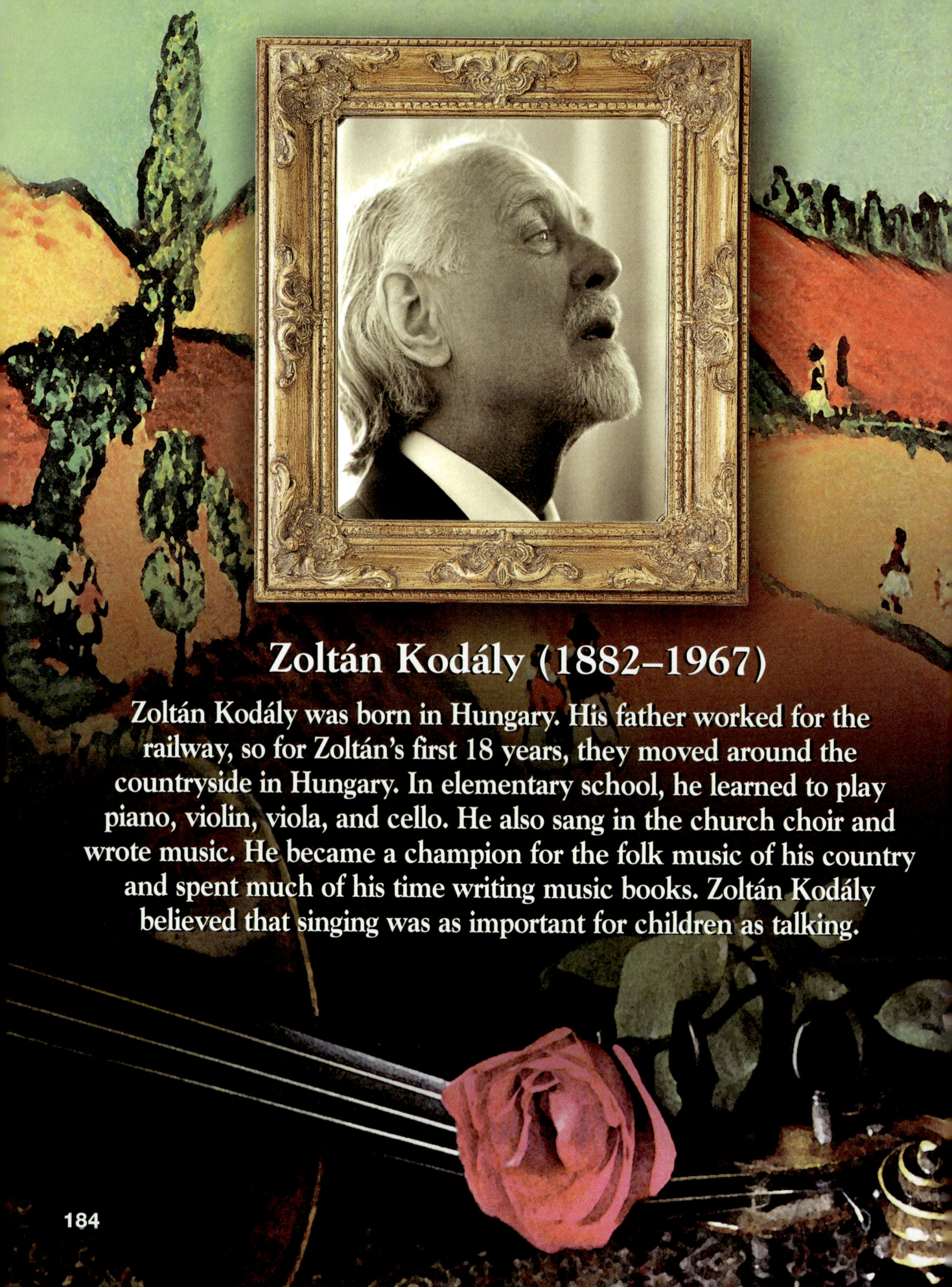

Zoltán Kodály (1882–1967)

Zoltán Kodály was born in Hungary. His father worked for the railway, so for Zoltán's first 18 years, they moved around the countryside in Hungary. In elementary school, he learned to play piano, violin, viola, and cello. He also sang in the church choir and wrote music. He became a champion for the folk music of his country and spent much of his time writing music books. Zoltán Kodály believed that singing was as important for children as talking.

Cuckoo Clock with squirrels and bird

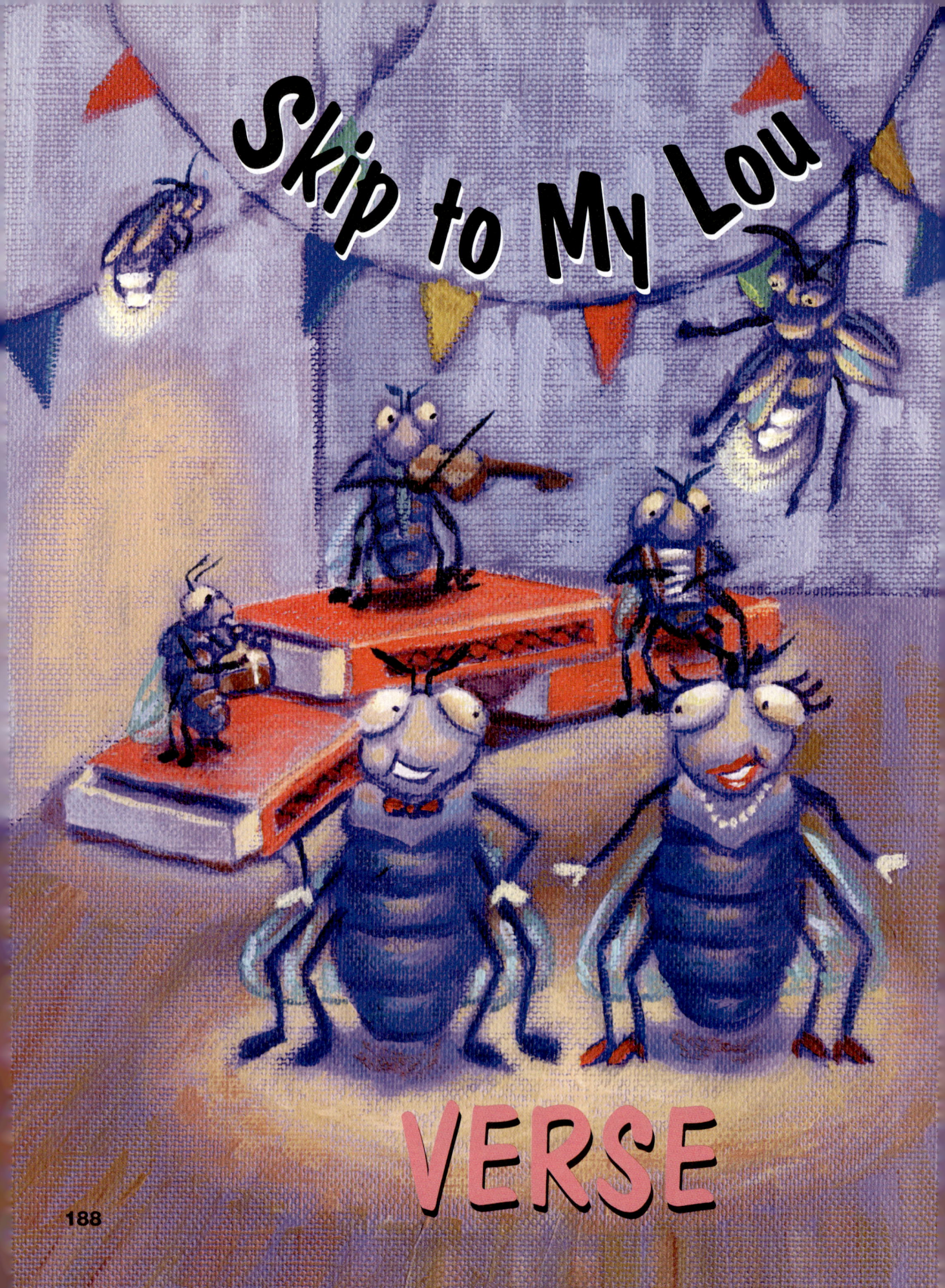

Shoo, Fly

Words by BILLY REEVES
Music by FRANK CAMPBELL
Arranged by JACK BULLOCK

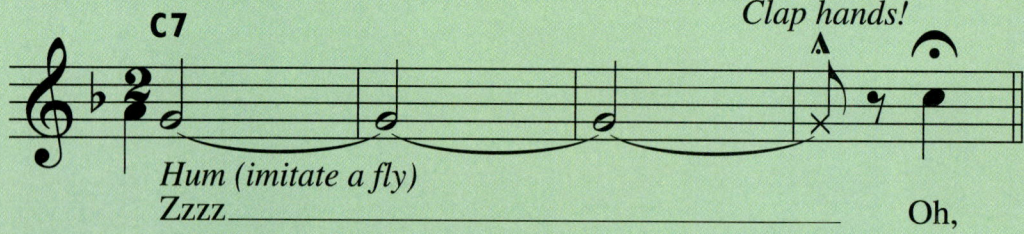

Hum (imitate a fly)
Zzzz_____ Oh,

shoo, fly! Don't both-er me;

shoo, fly! Don't both-er me.

Shoo, fly! Don't both-er me, for

I be-long to Comp-'ny G.

© 2003 BEAM ME UP MUSIC (ASCAP)   All Rights Administered by WARNER BROS. PUBLICATIONS U.S. INC.   All Rights Reserved

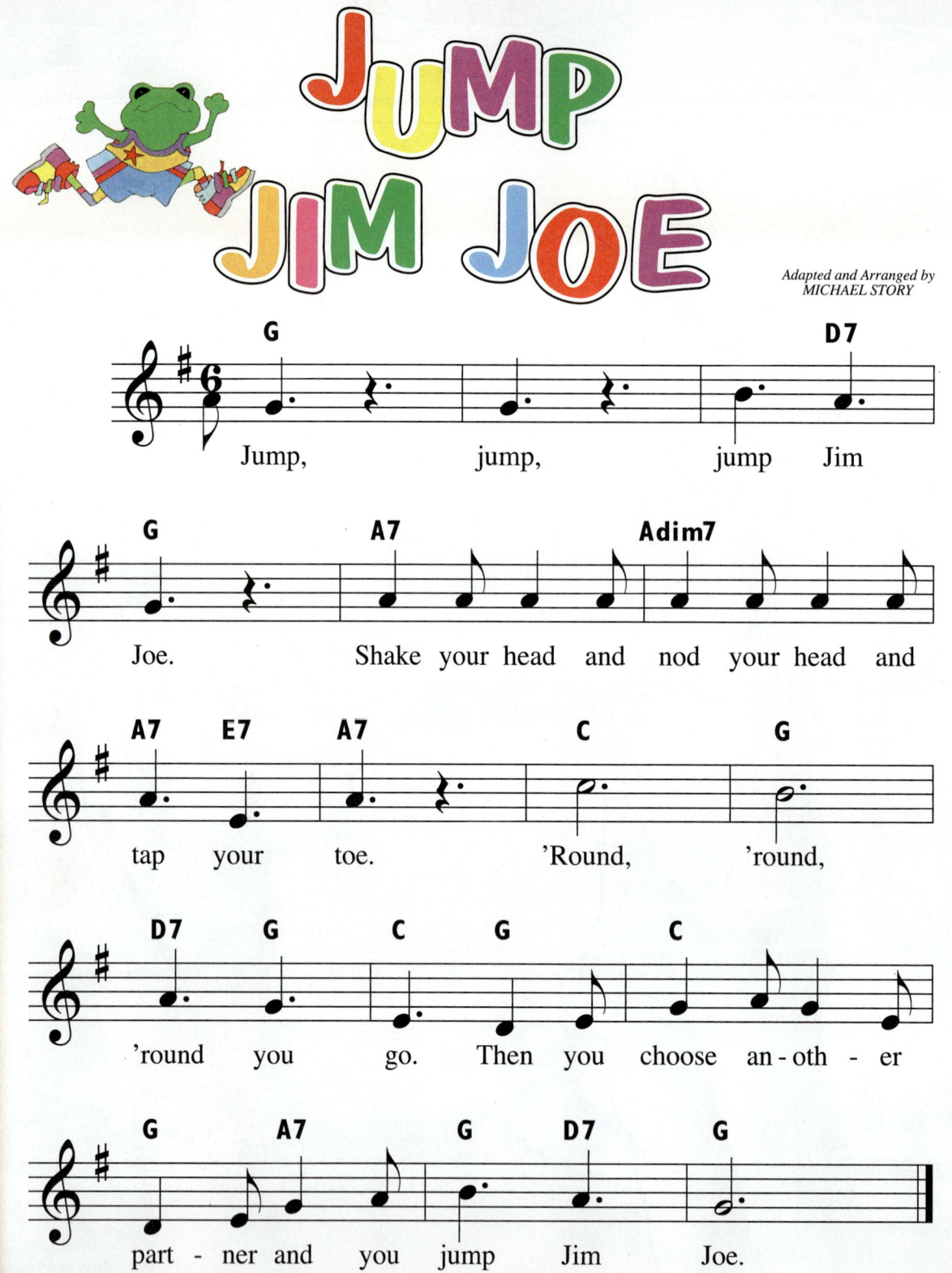

Jump, jump, jump Jim Joe.

Shake your head and nod your head and tap your toe.
'Round, 'round, 'round you go.

Then you choose another partner and you jump Jim Joe.

photo credit: Donald Norsworthy

Goodbye

Glossary

audience	A group that listens to or watches a performance
band	An instrumental ensemble, usually made up of wind and percussion instruments
bar line	The vertical line placed on a staff to divide the music into measures
call-and-response	A musical form in which the solo call is followed by a group response
chant	Text spoken rhythmically
chorus/choir	A group of singers
double bar line	Two vertical lines placed on the staff to indicate the end of a section or composition
downward	Melodic direction toward lower sounding pitches
echo	A repetition or imitation of another
eighth note	A note half the length of a quarter note or an eighth of the length of a whole note
fermata	A symbol that means to hold, pause
form	The order of sections in a music selection
half note	A note half the length of a whole note or twice the length of a quarter note
half-note dot	A note that equals three quarter notes; the dot lengthens the half note an additional half of its original value
improvise	Create music on the spot within guidelines
line note	A musical symbol with a staff line through its center
long tone	Sustained sound
mallet	A hammer-like device used to play a percussion instrument
melodic rhythm	The duration of tones; often, but not always, matches the rhythm of the words
melody	A series of musical phrases that express a composer's thoughts
ostinato	A repeated melodic or rhythmic pattern
pattern	The order of pitches/rhythms
phrase	A musical thought or idea
pitch	The highness or lowness of a tone
quarter note	A note half the length of a half note or a quarter the length of a whole note
quarter rest	A rest half the length of a half rest or a quarter the length of a whole rest
refrain	A short section of repeated material that occurs between verses
repeat sign	The symbol with two lines and two dots that means to perform a section or a composition again
repeated pattern	A pattern that occurs more than once
repeated tone	Tones that are the same and occur more than once
rest	The symbol for a silent unit of time
rhythm	The organization of sound and silence in time
short tone	Brief sound
skip	The distance from one tone to a tone that is more than a step away from it
solo	A performance by one person, with or without accompaniment
space note	A musical symbol written between staff lines
steady beat	The repeated even pulse of music
step	The distance from one tone to the tone next to it
tempo	The speed at which music is performed
tie	A curved line connecting two notes of the same pitch and played as if they were one
tone color	The sound that is special to each voice or instrument
unpitched	Without highness or lowness of sound
upward	Melodic direction toward higher sounding pitches
verse	A section of a song that reoccurs with different lyrics each time
whole note	A note equal to two half notes or four quarter notes

Index

Songs and Chants:
Ambos a Dos 122–123, 192–193
America .24–25
America, the Beautiful 52–53
Bate, Bate (chant) 19
Bingo 4–5
Cheki, Morena 166–167
Come and Sing 56–57, 72–73
Don Gato 152–153
Double Double Ice Ice (chant) . . .38–39, 46–47
El Gato y el Ratón 140–141
El Juego Chirimbolo 112–113
Get on Board 74–75
Going Over the Sea 178–179
Goodbye Song 10–11
Haak Gyo Jong 64–65
Hao Peng You 126–127
Hello Song 14–15
Hunt the Cows 66–67
Jump Jim Joe 32–33, 194–195
Lady, Lady .12
Li'l Liza Jane 96–97
Make New Friends 2
The Marvelous Toy 124–125
The Noble Duke of York 130–131
O, Susanna 100–101
Oats, Peas, Beans 136–137
Penny Song 162–163
Polly Wolly Doodle 80–81
Sally Go 'Round the Sun 168–169
Saute, Crapaud! 160–161
Shoo, Fly 48–49, 190–191
Skip to My Lou 60–61
Spanish Zoo Rhythms (chant) . . .148–149
Suo Gan 16–17
Ten in the Bed 84–85
This Old Man 20–21, 44–45
Tinga Layo 92–93
Yankee Doodle 26–27
You're a Grand Old Flag 28–29
Yum, Yum (chant) 40–41

MUSIC FOR LIFE

Music for Beauty:
Come and Sing 56–57, 72–73

Music for Beginnings:
Hello Song 14–15
Make New Friends 2

Music for Fun and Imagination:
Bingo 4–5
Don Gato 152–153
Double Double Ice Ice . . .38–39, 46–47
Going Over the Sea 178–179
The Marvelous Toy 124–125
The Noble Duke of York 130–131
Penny Song 162–163
Sally Go 'Round the Sun 168–169
This Old Man 20–21, 44–45

Music for Moving:
Cheki, Morena 166–167
Double Double Ice Ice . . .38–39, 46–47
El Juego Chirimbolo 112–113
Jump Jim Joe 32–33, 194–195
The Noble Duke of York 130–131
Oats, Peas, Beans 136–137
Penny Song 162–163
Sally Go 'Round the Sun 168–169
Ten in the Bed 84–85

Music for National Pride:
America .24–25
America, the Beautiful 122–123, 192–193
Yankee Doodle 26–27
You're a Grand Old Flag 28–29

Music From Many Regions:
Li'l Liza Jane 96–97
O, Susanna 100–101
Polly Wolly Doodle 80–81
Shoo, Fly 48–49, 190–191
Skip to My Lou 60–61

Music for Nature:
Don Gato 152–153
El Gato y el Ratón 140–41
Hunt the Cows 66–67
Oats, Peas, Beans 136–137
Saute, Crapaud! 160–161

Music for Other Learning:
Bingo 4–5
Double Double Ice Ice . . .38–39, 46–47
Going Over the Sea 178–179
Ten in the Bed 84–85

Music for the End of the Day:
Goodbye Song 10–11
Lady, Lady .12
Suo Gan 16–17
Ten in the Bed 84–85

Music for Working:
Going Over the Sea 178–179
Oats, Peas, Beans 136–137

Music From Many Nations:
Ambos a Dos 122–123, 192–193
Bate, Bate .19
Cheki, Morena 166–167
Don Gato 152–153
El Juego Chirimbolo 112–113
Haak Gyo Jong 64–65
Hao Peng You 126–127
Saute, Crapaud! 160–161
Suo Gan 16–17
Tinga Layo 92–93

Music for Travel:
Get on Board 74–75
Going Over the Sea 178–179
Sally Go 'Round the Sun 168–169

Music to Remember:
Lady, Lady .12
This Old Man 20–21, 44–45

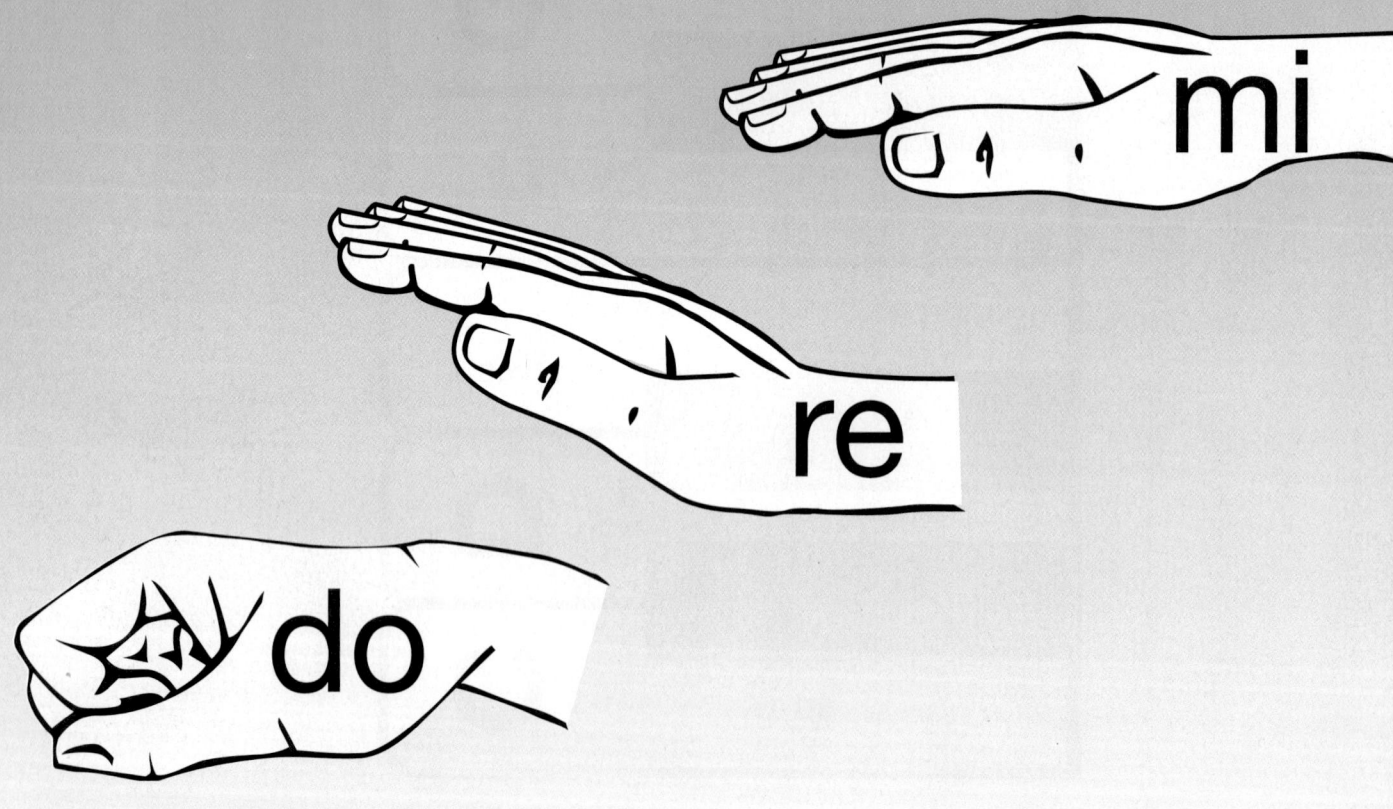

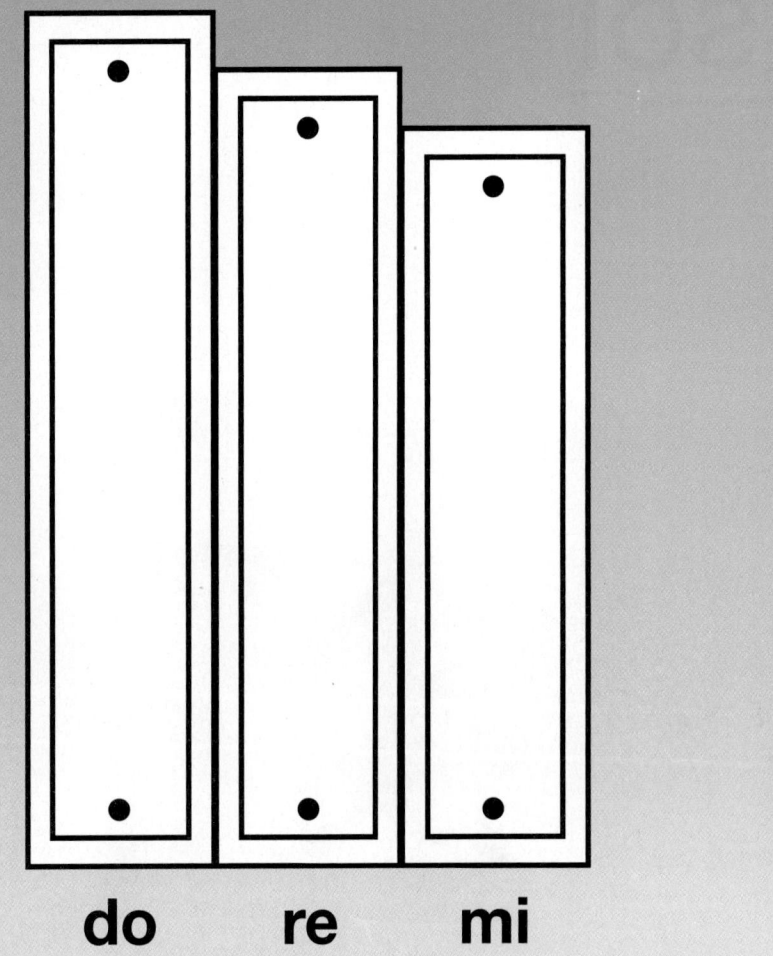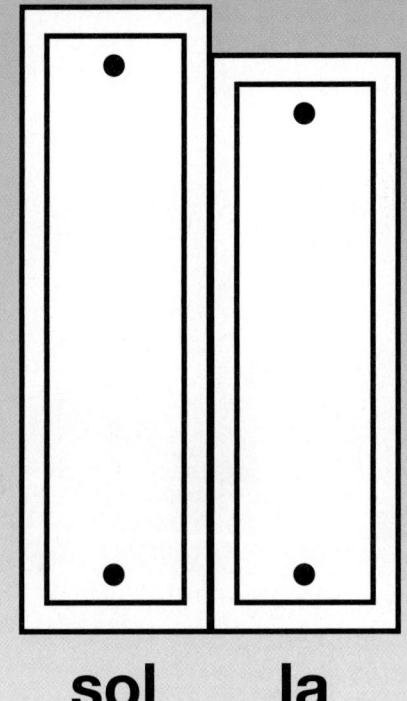